T0311526

The Birth of Grapevine Health

The COVID-19 pandemic has taught the world many things, but one of the most crucial is the need to communicate tailored health information through trusted messengers effectively. *The Birth of Grapevine Health* chronicles the experiences of one physician, Dr. Lisa Fitzpatrick, a CDC-trained medical epidemiologist on a mission to deliver trusted health information to the Black community through Grapevine Health, a community and health outreach organization she started with the aim to improve patient engagement and health literacy in underserved communities through the digital delivery of tailored health messages.

Fitzpatrick reveals why she began building an organization that, in 2020, appeared tailored for the COVID-19 pandemic long before that crisis unfolded across the globe. Frustrated by the lack of progress in addressing health inequity, Dr. Lisa moved into an under-resourced community to become proximal enough to better understand health inequity and the structural and policy changes needed to address it.

She weaves her professional experiences with storytelling and lessons learned into a call to action for healthcare leaders, decisionmakers, and funders to move beyond data collection and shift toward action to focus on health prevention, move our health support further upstream and, ultimately, improve health outcomes for underserved communities.

The Birth of Grapevine Health is part memoir, part health equity playbook, and offers a roadmap to actions needed to achieve health equity. At a time when health equity conversations seem ubiquitous, what sets *The Birth of Grapevine Health* apart is its embrace and integration of community voice. This book delivers deep insights and, at times, uncomfortable advice through the eyes of Black and brown patients and their communities about what it will take to achieve health equity.

The Birth of Grapevine Health

A Doctor's Journey to Build Trust and Restore Humanity in Medicine

Dr. Lisa K. Fitzpatrick

Routledge
Taylor & Francis Group
A PRODUCTIVITY PRESS BOOK

First published 2024
by Routledge
605 Third Avenue, New York, NY 10158

and by Routledge
4 Park Square, Milton Park, Abingdon, Oxon, OX14 4RN

Routledge is an imprint of the Taylor & Francis Group, an informa business

ISBN: 978-1-032-15298-1 (hbk)
ISBN: 978-1-032-15297-4 (pbk)
ISBN: 978-1-003-24350-2 (ebk)

DOI: 10.4324/9781003243502

Typeset in Garamond
by Deanta Global Publishing Services, Chennai, India

This book is dedicated to the community, my patients and community partners who teach me and humble me, and to Grapevine Health supporters everywhere.

Contents

Prologue

On a sunny fall day, I was standing outside a hospital with my organ model shooting a Dr. Lisa on the Street video when a woman who was just discharged from the hospital walked up and asked for my help. Dr. Lisa on the Street is my response to the healthcare system's failure to address low health literacy. It is a video series I created to capture people's attention and explain health and healthcare basics to people seeking answers to their health-related questions in plain language. That day I was shooting a video for a collaboration project with a health system about healthcare access. I asked people to share how they felt about telemedicine and their experiences, challenges and successes in obtaining primary care appointments. These conversations are always interesting, energizing, motivating and sometimes surprising. People feel comfortable revealing themselves, often in vulnerable ways. During the last interview that day, my peripheral vision captured a woman lingering near our videographer. Her gaze was focused on me. When we wrapped the shoot, she walked over to me and asked if I could help her understand her hospital discharge paperwork. A few minutes before she'd arrived and waited for me, she'd been discharged from the hospital. She was concerned because she still felt sick. She wanted to know if I could explain the instructions and help her understand what to do next. This is the responsibility of the hospital she'd

just left, yet she was discharged without a complete understanding of why she was hospitalized or how to proceed.
After I verified that she was granting me permission to review
her medical information, she handed me a wad of papers. I
peered at them for the discharge information. It was not there.
In that brief exchange, not only did she share her discharge
paperwork; she also handed me her insurance card and gave
me her phone number to text follow-up information. I thought
about how desperate she must be to wait patiently on the
street in order to seek help from a random doctor. She was
scared, desperate and didn't know where to turn, so she asked
a stranger. But to her I was not a complete stranger. I was a
Black doctor standing on the street answering people's questions and listening to their concerns. To her, I was a trusted
messenger.

The brief encounter can serve as a use case for several
timely and controversial matters in healthcare innovation and
healthcare system transformation. These include: the concept
of hard-to-reach or unreachable people, underinsurance, lopsided access to care, trust, health literacy, health equity, innovation constraints imposed by the Health Insurance Portability
and Accountability Act (HIPAA), interpretation, the digital
divide, cultural competency and humanity in healthcare. Right
there on the street in those moments talking with her, each
of these issues were relevant, and the opportunities to impact
and influence healthcare outcomes were staring back at me.
She was not hard to reach or unreachable. She walked right
up to me and asked for help. Why? Based on my accessibility,
availability and her perceived openness to me, she trusted me.
Despite being surrounded by healthcare providers the previous
forty-eight hours, she believed I would help her understand
what was happening with her health and why she would be
discharged despite her symptoms. Not only did she trust me
at that moment, she also shared personal health information
with me and gave me her smartphone number and permission

to communicate with her via text message. I asked why she waited to talk to me, and she said because I seemed like I was willing to listen and might be able to help. She was a Black woman, insured by Medicaid. I wondered how many people like her across the US were struggling in the same way as she was. Over the years I had heard many stories like hers— people feeling dismissed, unheard, disrespected because of zip code, insurance type, diction, skin color or the number of zeroes in their bank account. These are people left feeling confused, ignored and with questions unanswered. The volume of stories like these have compelled me to use my gifts to serve people from underserved and under-resourced communities. For the past four years I have been building a company that focuses on the digital delivery of tailored and culturally appropriate health information to underserved communities by trusted messengers. As part of Grapevine Health, we film and upload videos of Dr. Lisa on the Street as well as additional segments like Ask the Doctor. We use video, YouTube, word of mouth and more recently text messaging to answer questions from the community and combat the spread of misinformation. Data show that this type of direct community engagement lowers costs for insurance companies and taxpayers while improving quality of life for patients. When people understand health information and trust those delivering the messages, they are more likely to seek preventive care and better manage and even prevent chronic health conditions.

Recently a woman called me to learn more about what we do at Grapevine Health. Freshly attuned to Black Americans' distrust of healthcare and the health disparities thrust into the spotlight during the pandemic, she asked if the company was born in response to the pandemic. Surprised to hear Grapevine Health was born in 2019, *before* the pandemic, she referred to me as an oracle. It is not a deserving title. This is the need I saw most clearly in 2013 when I started talking to strangers on the street. But looking back it was there all along, for decades, plainly confronting not just me but all of us. We chose not to see it or act on it. There were cries for help; pleas for support to navigate a sea of overwhelming and complicated information; longing and craving for access to trusted health information. I am now simply responding to what I was seeing and hearing in the community all along.

People also ask why a mid-career doctor on a successful career trajectory would leave traditional medicine, healthcare leadership and lucrative employment opportunities and risk starting a company focused on something they perceive as mundane as health education and health communication for the poor and underserved. My answer is that I had to. Despite my tenure at important organizations like the Centers for Disease Control and Prevention, Medicaid, academic institutions and health systems, there was always a restlessness in me, believing and wondering if we could be more impactful if we followed the voice of the community and created for them and with them. I did not begin with entrepreneurial aspirations or the desire to build a company. Over the years, patient and community encounters taught me how people wanted to receive help navigating their health. But my roles in the public sector and safety net institutions did not afford me access to the infrastructure or financial resources needed to support underserved communities and address their needs in real time, in a moment of crisis or when a health concern was sharply in focus. I saw these as missed opportunities to make a connection, build trust and engage in their health.

My purpose is validated every time I meet someone on the street, and now via videoconference, who is simply seeking trusted, non-judgmental health information from someone who understands their journey. Grapevine Health's mission is validated by each encounter with someone who is confused, afraid or discouraged about their health and unsure how to navigate it or the healthcare system. I am convinced people are craving access to easily accessible, no BS, credible, relatable and trustworthy health information.

The truth is Grapevine Health should be a public service embedded within authoritative health institutions like the Centers for Disease Control, the Center for Medicaid and Medicare Services or the Department of Health and Human Services. But these organizations tend to be too bureaucratic to rapidly generate tailored health information and communication in a moment of need. Most of the time, people don't think about their health and don't want to. But moments arise when a person needs real-time information to make a health decision. Grapevine Health is my response to this need.

This book is about how I came to know what I know about the need for trusted health information and patient engagement. It also invites you to understand how I learned about the need for more humanity in medicine from patients, community members, and even my own experiences with the healthcare system. This book helps you understand why and how I built Grapevine Health and what the future of healthcare and health equity can look like from a community-centered approach.

Overall, Grapevine Health is the culmination of thirty years of experience in healthcare, learning from patients and community members and partnering with social service organizations. We are on a path to delivering a service for communities that need access to trusted health information most—on their terms, not ours. This book, part professional memoir, part health equity playbook, shares what my quest to improve health literacy has taught me about communities, patient engagement, social drivers of health outcomes and the dire need for more humanity in healthcare. Above all, my path to Grapevine Health can show us all a bit about what it will take to address health inequity once and for all.

Part 1

Health Literacy Matters

Do the best you can until you know better. Then
when you know better, do better.

Maya Angelou

Knowledge itself is power.

Sir Francis Bacon

I know exactly when I became keenly aware of my passion
for health literacy and for sharing the knowledge people need
to manage their body and health. It was 2007. I was a panel-
ist for a community event sponsored by 100 Black Men[1] in
Atlanta, Georgia. I was invited by a medical school class-
mate and now renowned heart surgeon, Dr. William Cooper.[2]
William felt that the panel needed a community voice to
complement the esteemed academicians and seasoned health
policy leaders. My co-panelists were a researcher, epidemiologist and scholar on health and racism, the head of chronic
diseases for the Centers for Disease Control and Prevention
(CDC), a former US assistant secretary for health and a former
surgeon general. After panel remarks, the moderator turned
to the audience for questions. As we each took turns answering the questions, something happened that I had not fully

DOI: 10.4324/9781003243502-1   1 appreciated until the program was over. I had listened as my co-panelists described their work in academic terms peppered with health policy jargon. When it was my turn to speak, I used plain language to describe my work at CDC. When the time came for audience questions, I kept my responses relatable and avoided medical and public health jargon. As I walked off the stage a line of people had formed to speak to me. The question I will never forget came from a Black man in his sixties who asked, "How does someone like *me* access someone like *you* on a regular basis?" He told me he had a doctor who was treating his high blood pressure, but he didn't believe everything his doctor said and didn't understand why he needed to be on medication. That moment is the true origin of Grapevine Health,[3] a company I would establish twelve years later to help people like him make sense of medical information. He was asking me how to find a trusted health messenger to help demystify the information he was getting about his health. I have heard variations of his question from friends, family, patients and people on the street.

That moment has stayed with me and served as a compass for my work. Looking back, I always cared about helping people understand health information and still believe knowledge is the gateway to better health. For years, I have been bombarded by questions from people who crave explanations about health, medical jargon, healthcare, research and the human body. From the time my ten-year-old cousin asked me during my second year of medical school to explain why he got a headache in a specific spot of his head to 2001, standing on the floor of the Brentwood Post Office in Washington, DC, allaying fears about Anthrax for frightened postal workers, I realized I was pretty good at demystifying health information. I didn't realize just how good until the 100 Black Men event. Confusion about health information is an unspoken epidemic, and it leads to preventable disease, suffering, death[4] and financial waste.[5] No one should suffer or die simply because they do not have answers to questions about their health. And so, this has become my life's mission—to provide trusted, relatable and understandable health information to people who need it most, in the moment they need it.

A few years ago a friend told me about a relative who was fighting for her life in the intensive care unit (ICU). She had collapsed at work and was rushed to the emergency room. The woman was diagnosed with a preventable bloodstream infection that damaged a heart valve and required open heart surgery. She spent ten days in the ICU. The hospital bill was over a million dollars. The source of the infection was an infected tooth. She had never had a dental exam and was unaware of the connection between physical health and dental health. This is why health literacy matters.

The Case for Health Literacy

Health literacy is defined by the National Academy of Medicine[6] as: "The degree to which individuals have the capacity to obtain, process, and understand basic health information and services needed to make appropriate health decisions."[7] Over the years there have been many iterations of this definition, but practically speaking, people need to understand how their bodies work, what to look for to know when something goes wrong, what to do about it and when to seek help.

Limited health literacy[8] is costly and transcends race, income and class. A recent study from the University of Minnesota shows confusing medical jargon even transcends education level.[9]

However, data show people from poorer socioeconomic backgrounds and with low background literacy suffer the most negative impacts from limited health literacy.[10] Lower health literacy is consistently linked to poor health outcomes.[11] Research data also show that people with limited health literacy have higher death rates,[12] are less engaged in primary care, use the emergency room more often and have difficulty reading prescription labels, which leads to avoidable healthcare expenditures. If health literacy has such a profound impact on health outcomes,[13] why then have we failed to embrace it as a social driver of health? More importantly, why are we not prioritizing and investing in interventions to address it along with other social drivers of health like food, housing, transportation and employment?

Health systems and insurance companies spend millions to produce health information content, which is often ignored by patients and healthcare consumers. In 2019 over thirty billion dollars was spent on health communication for consumers.[14] What might be achieved if we spent even a tenth of that on strategies to improve health literacy?

Over the years my engagement with patients and community members has highlighted several actions capable of improving low health literacy and its impact on health outcomes, particularly for underserved and under-resourced communities.

First, we can recognize and address the association between health literacy and trust in healthcare. Without the appropriate support, the complex language of health and healthcare can be intimidating, confusing and incomprehensible. Failure to recognize and intervene in health literacy challenges further erodes trust and contributes to poor engagement in care.[15] Limited health literacy is often linked to distrust and, in part, can be addressed by community-based outreach and engagement. This approach facilitates a better understanding of cultural and social influencers of health behavior, which can be used to design messaging.

Second, we should understand low health literacy is not a one-size-fits-all designation. For some the challenge is language, for others it is health system navigation for multiple chronic health conditions and for still others it may be challenges with numeracy and understanding how and when to take medication. For example, if a prescription is written "twice a day," this might be interpreted as two times a day or two pills a day for someone with low health literacy. A colleague informed me that a prescription reading "once a day" could be misconstrued by a Spanish-speaking patient with health literacy challenges and low English literacy as eleven pills a day or eleven *times* a day because in Spanish "once" means eleven.

Third, we must embrace and deeply understand how limited health literacy influences health outcomes and commit to addressing this problem. We must value health literacy enough to establish it as an actionable social driver of poor health outcomes alongside others like transportation, food and housing. This means better quantifying the costs of limited health literacy and its contribution to avoidable healthcare expenditures. A recent systematic review[16] suggested an association between health disparities and low health literacy. However, the authors concluded that the evidence for the association was limited due to variations in study approaches and a lack of specificity about the health disparities in question.[17] Data establishing the association between low health literacy and specific health outcomes exist, and these should be mined and analyzed to provide unequivocal support for establishing health literacy as an explicit social driver of health outcomes. The truth is, although health literacy is a known contributor to health inequity,[18] we don't value it as a powerful driver of health outcomes and expenditures. If we did, we would invest in it and diligently explore more effective ways to identify and measure it.

Finally, we should tailor health education and information content to ensure it is relevant for those who need it. If corporations can effectively brand and market products to engage and establish an emotional connection with their consumers, why is the healthcare industry fearful of such branding[19] and failing to do the same? For example, according to McKinsey, many health insurers have been slow to fully embrace social media as a major component of their health education and communication strategies, despite knowing it is the primary source of information for many of their enrollees.[20] Accepting the risk of doing so may help address the unmitigated costs associated with emergency room overuse and avoidable hospital admissions.[21]

In health, medicine and healthcare, health literacy touches everything. We will never eliminate health disparities without informed, engaged patients and communities. We will never adequately diversify clinical trials without people understanding the purpose, power and promise of scientific research and the need for their participation. We will never create healthier, prevention-focused communities unless people understand how to make better health decisions. Despite this, health literacy is often dismissed and overlooked as an influencer of health outcomes and engagement in healthcare. People need to understand how to engage in healthcare, when and how their insurance works and what to do to maintain good health. I think of health literacy as an umbrella concept under which falls practical knowledge and understanding across many domains pertinent to health, including medication literacy and disease-specific literacy, for example HIV literacy, diabetes literacy or hepatitis literacy. Even nutrition literacy deserves specific attention. Years ago, a member of one of my clinical teams said, "Dr. Fitzpatrick, I always hear about eating healthy but what does that mean? When I go to the grocery store I don't know what I am supposed to buy so I just buy what I like." Soon after, I shopped with a few members of an underserved community and realized my teammate was not alone. I identified vegetables for people and taught them about food labels, how to read them and why they were important. I explained the difference between carbohydrates, fats and proteins and assisted in identifying which foods contained added sugars. As a component of health literacy, food literacy[22] should be prioritized because food insecurity has emerged as a critical healthcare policy issue. Now recognized as a social determinant of health (SDOH),[23] the field has received unprecedented attention and investment, primarily in the form of tailored meal delivery. Food as medicine programs[24] and support have also emerged at renowned institutions like Geisinger[25] and Elevance Health Foundation.[26] Evaluation of some of these programs has even shown a statistically significant benefit.[27] However, what is missing and critical for the sustainability and long-term health impact of many of these types of programs is nutrition literacy. Do people understand the impact of food and food choices on their health? Do they understand what to buy and how to prepare food? Do they have the equipment needed to prepare food? Written recipes are abundant, but what difficulty might someone with low reading ability have with following a recipe?

Beyond nutrition literacy, my interactions and research in underserved communities highlight how woefully inadequate the healthcare system, particularly providers, has become in the delivery of health information in plain language.

Whether at community events, a bedside or while reading text messages on my phone, I repeatedly see the ways we are failing to equip communities with relatable, actionable information in a language that is meaningful to them. I encountered this during a clinical consultation. I was asked to consult on a hospitalized surgical patient. I remember standing at the bedside and realizing the gentleman had no idea why he was having surgery. He knew it had something to do with his circulation but beyond that could not articulate much about his disease or the need for surgical intervention. Failure to communicate in plain language is a failure of the health system and the healthcare provider. But, somehow, the way we communicate about health literacy tends to be judgmental and often blames the person who needs our help. We talk about health literacy as a patient deficit when instead a person's inability to understand what we say reflects our inadequacy in delivering the support people need.

Sometimes, rather than subject themselves to our jargon, medicalese and inadequate communication, people—our patients—avoid us, delay care and only return, usually to the emergency room, under duress when their only choice is healthcare or death.

Once I asked a man why he waited so long to be seen for a longstanding medical issue that landed him in the hospital for twenty-three days; he said, "I try to avoid doctors and hospitals if I can help it." The place was a mystery to him, and it made him feel lost at sea. This is neglect. It is a neglect of our duty to demystify health information, allay fear and arm people with the information they need to take lifesaving health actions.

Providing people with credible, trusted health information can also alleviate a powerful driver of engagement in healthcare—fear. Fear impacts willingness to engage in healthcare. We have enough data to show a more health-literate person is a healthier person. However, the messages must be tailored and delivered by a trusted messenger, which, whether we like it or not, is often word of mouth, person to person—the grapevine.

After everything I have learned over the years about humanity, health behaviors, health-related decision making and the need for relatable, understandable health information, I wanted my entrepreneurial adventure to tackle the grapevine. I wanted to focus on the delivery of trusted information to demystify health language and communication in ways that complemented and competed with the grapevine. After hearing hundreds of people on the street say things like the man at the 100 Black Men event all those years ago—"No one has ever explained it that way," or, "Thanks for breaking it down for me like that"—I knew there was a need and a hunger for better health communication. I also knew I had a gift and I wanted to use it to help close healthcare communication gaps for underserved communities and improve health literacy. If health literacy is the ability to understand and use health information to become healthier, the fundamental problem I wanted my company to solve was reliance on the grapevine for health information, particularly for Medicaid patients.

Health Information on the Grapevine

Limited health literacy has been studied for decades and is known to be correlated with poorer health outcomes, higher costs of care and less engagement in care. Thus, relying on the grapevine for health information can lead to and exacerbate low health literacy. For example, medication sharing[28] among friends and family is linked to the grapevine. This practice requires community members to self-diagnose themselves and others and intuit the safety in taking a medication prescribed for someone else. This can be harmful but is preventable through effective health communication.

Over the years, patients have shared their rationale for sharing medications and self-diagnosing based on their interpretations of physician instructions. A patient once told me he stopped taking his medication because he didn't "feel" anything when he took the pill so he believed it was not working. Similarly, another patient informed me he wanted to avoid his monthly medication co-pay so he lengthened the duration of his medication by taking a pill every other day rather than every day as prescribed. In these cases, making time to explain the medication pharmacology, physiology and rationale in plain language shifted their understanding and consequently their medication adherence.

I have learned people invent narratives about their health that align with their perceptions about how the body works.

Some seek validation from trusted sources, like friends and family, to endorse their behavior. An antidote to this tendency can be credible, relatable health information. I have also asked people how they determine if health information is true. A woman who ingests health information on social media told me, "It's about the likes. If you got a lot of likes you must be doing something right. Otherwise, why would so many people follow you and like you?"

On the street and in the clinic I have heard a lot of misinformation gone wrong on the grapevine like:

> "Once you start a medication you can never come off."
> "Once you have AIDS that's it, you die."
> "Peeing on the ground gives you a stye on your eye."
> "Walking outside with wet hair gives you walking pneumonia."
> "Bacon fat and ear wax can diagnose a sexually transmitted disease."

The table in the Appendix lists questions I have received from friends, family and the public about medicine, science and public health that highlight the impact of our failure to prioritize health literacy interventions to improve health and mitigate the mental health impact of low health literacy.

The evolution of health information on the grapevine can be like the game of telephone. As the information is passed from person to person and group to group, over time the message becomes distorted, sometimes beyond recognition. This is the life cycle of a lot of health misinformation. Misinformation is not always intentional but rather a misinterpretation or misperception of factual, verifiable information.

While attending a community meeting about self-care, health and wellness, I eagerly awaited the keynote speaker.

She had self-published a book about her journey to wellness after emerging from a life of poverty. When she spoke about the importance of nutrition, I was stunned by a comment she confidently made about sugar. She said, "Every time you eat sugar, your immune system shuts down for five hours." I knew this was not true but was curious about why she thought so. I conducted a literature search and found a research study[29] from the 1970s that assessed the association between sugar and immunity. In this study, the researchers gave mice sugar and studied the reaction in different components of the immune system. In the study, the researchers noticed the macrophages were sluggish for five hours. Our immune systems contain macrophages which run around picking up and getting rid of garbage and debris in our cells. Macrophages are only one component of the immune system, and their sluggishness is certainly not equivalent to the impact of something like chemotherapy or a bone marrow transplant, both of which "shut down the immune system."

Bad health information is everywhere, but if presented with authority from a person who appears credible the information takes off on the grapevine like wildfire. I've learned over the years that a lot of health misinformation is not malicious. Truthful information on the grapevine can become distorted and devolve into misinformation. People are doing their best to interpret the information they read from disparate sources on the Internet. They create a narrative that makes sense to them and it becomes gospel.

After accumulating a body of knowledge directly from the community for over a decade, the relevance and opportunity for Grapevine Health became crystal clear to me. I launched Grapevine Health in 2019 as a way for people to access trusted, accessible and culturally appropriate information and increase their healthcare literacy. While I always knew this work was important, in less than a year I would learn just how relevant, urgent and necessary it was to bring accurate health information directly to our communities as the COVID-19 pandemic emerged. I would also soon learn that addressing health misinformation requires a war chest because efforts to combat it feel like an endless game of whack-a-mole.

Health Information: The Gateway to Engagement

Health information is ubiquitous and abundant. In fact, it is so abundant that it's often dismissed as irrelevant in addressing health equity. A few years ago, a senior leader at a health system told me he didn't think the world needed more health information content because we had more content than we needed. To him the problem was, instead, Internet access. If people could freely access the Internet, they would have everything they need to obtain the resources and information they need to improve their health. Over the years, I have engaged in thousands of discussions about the importance of tailored, culturally appropriate, relatable health information and have often encountered variations on this perspective. I was told, "Information is not enough." Indeed, relatable, jargon-free, culturally appropriate health information is not a panacea to eliminate health disparities—but neither are electronic health records, interoperability and big data analytics. These interventions must work together to create an accessible, usable system, none of which matters if we don't have people motivated and engaged in their own health. And what is the gateway to engagement? Information.

But the information must be tailored, delivered via the right channel and at the moment a person needs it. For underserved Black communities, we have not invested enough time, resources and energy into addressing health information needs. For example, during a discussion group with Black diabetes patients, toward the end of the discussion, a man who had been living with diabetes for seven years asked, "I thought I heard someone say diabetes can affect the kidney. Is that true and can you talk about that?" A Google search would certainly answer his question. There were also several people in his immediate circle with diabetes, yet the information had not traveled to him. Why hadn't it? Similarly, my team encountered a woman at a health fair with dangerously high blood pressure. When I followed up to help get her linked to primary care services, I told her my concerns about and the dangers of walking around with such high and untreated blood pressure.

I asked, "Aren't you having headaches? Are you having trouble with your vision?" She said, "I have been having these headaches for years but I figured it was just stress from minding these grandkids."

She said her vision had been blurry for a while, but she figured she needed glasses and had planned to see an eye doctor. I convinced her to seek care immediately, and she accessed the services she needed. Her health literacy was low about her condition, and she told me she was unaware of the association between high blood pressure and eye disease. Given the abundance of available health information content about heart disease, high blood pressure and strokes, how had this information escaped her or not crossed her health information pathways? Did she encounter it and not understand it? Did the messages not resonate or feel relevant to her? Every year, nearly seven hundred thousand people die from cardiovascular diseases that are largely preventable.[30] While it is true that information alone will not address these disparities, without the right information, delivered in the right way by the right messenger, interventions like early diagnostics and preventive treatment may never be sought or obtained in underserved communities.

Preparing the Community to Use Health Information

The power of addressing health literacy is in equipping patients and communities to communicate with health systems and healthcare providers and to advocate for themselves. In healthcare there is a paternalistic, lopsided, hierarchical power dynamic. People are reluctant to engage in healthcare because it is a relationship rife with demands, judgment and expectations but short on acceptance, empathy and, ironically, humanity. In a discussion group, a woman told us her primary care visits felt like punishment and she did not want to be chastised for not following the doctor's orders. She said she knew she needed to lose weight and going to the doctor and hearing about this in judgmental tones over and over made her feel bad about herself, so she stopped going.

Within the patient–provider relationship, we offer a lot of instructions—"take this," "go there," "do that." Everything is on our terms and according to our timelines and systems. This is the reason we expect people to wait when we are running late but feel emboldened enough to deny care and ask a person to reschedule if they are late for their appointment. We have structured these systems to serve people but fail to see the hypocrisy in subjecting people to judgmental, inflexible systems that lack empathy. We prioritize process over people rather than finding the balance between the two.

Addressing health literacy can prepare people to engage with this imperfect system.

One day while I was out in the community talking to people about cancer screening, a woman told me:

> "This is good information. I wanted to ask my doctor these kinds of questions but he didn't have time."
> I said, "You should always ask questions, especially if you don't understand something."
> She said, "Really? You can do that? I had no idea."

People have these perceptions because research shows healthcare providers spend the majority of the visit time talking rather than listening.[31] Ways to improve health literacy to support patient advocacy include education about symptoms, disease basics and specific questions to ask. Having specific information can also encourage patients to speak up when their intuition and instincts suggest something is amiss, whether neglect, bias, racism or misdiagnosis.

I encountered a situation like this as a patient when I was fourteen years old. Nowadays racism is openly spoken about as a hallmark of healthcare delivery. But as a fourteen-year-old in the eighties, shielded by naiveté, I knew nothing about it. I was a junior high school student living in St. Louis and had developed a rash on my chest and back. I went to see a doctor who referred me to another doctor for a second opinion. I don't remember the details of how I came to sit at the table of the second doctor, but what I remember so vividly is a male doctor coming in to look at my rash and asking only a few questions. He left the room and came back with another older, male doctor who, without uttering a word, looked at my rash. They traded a few comments, and the first doctor said to the second, "Should I send her?" The older doctor turned toward me, still silent, this time peering into my eyes, his gaze fixed upon me and said, "Yeah, I would send her." The first doctor wrote something on a prescription pad and sent me to have blood drawn. I later learned I was tested for syphilis. I wasn't even sexually active, but I guess these doctors decided they could tell by looking at me. Only in hindsight would I understand how these doctors were making decisions without full information while disbelieving and dismissing my concerns and explanations for my symptoms. It would take me many years after medical training to fully understand how rampant paternalism and racism are in medicine and just how one-sided the doctor–patient relationship really is. If I had understood how the system worked, maybe I would have spoken up—albeit a tall order for a teen.

Another example of the need to arm people with lifesaving information is from my internal medicine residency, long before I understood the importance of public health, population health or health literacy. I was on a pathology (study of the causes of death) rotation and had an encounter that stays with me because it has become central to my efforts to improve health literacy. I was watching an autopsy. The victim's aorta—the giant artery running through the middle of the body that offshoots all the other blood vessels—had been spliced open and was splayed across the table. The coroner pointed to a bright yellow film covering the length of the artery and called it an incidental finding, meaning it was not what killed him. He quizzed me, "Do you know what that is?"

It looked as if someone had taken a ladle and spread a fine layer of butter inside the lining of his artery. I stared wondering but had no idea and could not imagine what it could be.

He informed me, "That's hardening of the arteries. He's got atherosclerosis."

As I stared at the artery and then at the accident victim on the table, I was shocked. I couldn't believe my eyes or process this information. Perhaps you are wondering why a doctor would be so dumbfounded by the finding of atherosclerosis at an autopsy in our society so plagued with bad food, diabetes, heart disease and so many other preventable health conditions. It is because this victim with the butter-laden vessel was only six years old.

A wealth of data exists from autopsies showing heart disease as incidental findings in people of all ages, and we know unequivocally that the process of atherosclerosis begins early in life. This means prevention through healthy food and consistent exercise is our best chance to prevent long-term morbidity and mortality from heart disease. However, these data and experiences are rarely, if at all, discussed with the general public. Cardiovascular or heart disease remains the leading cause of death in the US. And it is preventable. But like then and even more now, we have made it more accessible and convenient to engage in a heart disease-inducing lifestyle than in one that prevents high blood pressure, heart attacks, strokes, kidney failure and limb amputations.

Our neglect to sufficiently educate, prioritize prevention and support young people to avoid these health hazards in front of them is among our greatest national failures. But it isn't too late for health literacy interventions.

Understanding Community

One of my most consistently rewarding pursuits in health-care has been community engagement. I have volunteered for community outreach and Ask the Doctor sessions on behalf of hospitals and have made appearances on television, radio and at church events to deliver health education. In the years before I started Grapevine Health, I knew this was my zone of genius and it is still where I thrive. But it is humbling. The community teaches me what people know and understand about their health and how the health system works. Being on the street, answering questions and educating others makes me come alive. On the street and in the community I have heard about why people delay care, and it almost always involves some element of money, fear, distrust or time. I can often see the relief my explanations offer, especially if the person has been harboring the question or fear for a while but was unsure where to turn.

Community engagement has also shown me just how terri-fied people can be of their bodies and the potential for their bodies to turn against them. I saw—and still see—my health education efforts as a soothing salve delivering peace of mind. I learned most concerns people have about their bodies are rooted in misunderstanding and conflicting information. Once I explained how the body worked, I could see a wave of calm flow over them. The more engaged I was, the more my conviction grew about the need to enable access to trusted, relatable health information from Black doctors.

Dr. Lisa on the Street

The months and years following my interaction at the 100 Black Men event created a restlessness in me about scaling my talent to reach Black people who were seeking a trusted health messenger. I started thinking about how to use technology to scale my health communication ability. The problem was, I was not tech savvy. CDC had issued me a BlackBerry and I barely knew how to use it. In fact, although mobile phones were the rage in the early 2000s, I'd often forget I had one. One day I had to pick my cousin up at the airport and I wasted almost an hour driving around trying to find him. I apologized profusely when he got in the car and he said, "Why didn't you just call my cell phone?" The phone was in the side pocket, turned off, and it had never occurred to me to use it. This is the reason it took me several years to launch Dr. Lisa on the Street. I was busy working to pay my bills and at that time could not see a path to democratizing my voice through technology to help people like the man at the 100 Black Men event.

Then in 2012, I saw a clip from Jay Leno's Jaywalking.[32] In the segment, Leno walks around LA asking people basic questions about things like history and politics. People get the questions wrong, and the audience laughs. While my goal wasn't to poke fun at anyone, I wondered if an edutainment approach might help me democratize trusted health information. Leno had the right idea about how to reach and connect with people outside the TV studio in a way that's accessible and entertaining. If I wanted to connect with people directly too, I knew where to find them: on street corners, outside grocery stories, at the National Mall and anywhere folks gathered.

I did not know how to best implement my plan, especially while I still needed to pay my bills. Until one day I attended a community meeting at my local bike shop. The meeting opened with a video. I was struck by the video quality and storytelling displayed in the piece, so I asked the bike shop owner about the creator. He introduced me to Francis Tatem. Francis was a twenty-something recent journalism grad, videographer, storyteller and freelancer. I met with him soon after. He interviewed me and I told him my vision. I wanted to use community voice, conversations and shared experiences to educate people about health, healthcare and engagement with healthcare providers. We decided the best next step was to go out onto the street and see what happened. Our first creation was about the flu.[33] We asked people questions about the flu and flu vaccines and educated them using accessible language without talking down or using jargon. When I saw Francis's first edit, I knew we were on to something. Dr. Lisa on the Street was born. Our next video was about doctor–patient communication.[34] Francis housed the video on YouTube, and even though I didn't yet have a formal YouTube channel it accumulated over two thousand views and I received nearly a dozen emails from academics asking if they could use my video in the classroom.

I've heard some pretty incredible things on the street. In fact, I think street walking and talking should become a prerequisite for medical, nursing, dental and pharmacy school graduation. Walking the streets taught me about how universally challenging it is to navigate the health system or find convenient access to dignified, respectful healthcare at the moment you need it. When I started Dr. Lisa on the Street, I approached people from all backgrounds and socioeconomic classes. I had no trouble getting a variety of people to talk to me. Some people, rather than asking questions, only wanted to share and vent about their healthcare horror stories. Thus, Dr. Lisa on the Street also became part impromptu therapist. I realized people just wanted to be heard. I encountered many emotions and reactions to being on the street, including joy, humility, gratitude, surprise and hope. The universal appeal of Dr. Lisa on the Street meant I had an idea that could engage the public and that I could potentially scale digitally. Francis and I continued to produce episodes of Dr. Lisa on the Street and post them to YouTube. Our efforts over the next few years continued to be random, though, because we did not yet have the funding or the vision for how to pursue this as a larger health literacy intervention while I was still working full-time. Yet it was clear there was interest in my initiative. People on the streets asked us to make more videos and answer more questions, and I spoke to experts in the media who thought the idea of a Dr. Lisa on the Street enterprise was interesting. But they believed the way to success was through television as a medical contributor, whereas my goal was to be in the street connecting directly with people and patients. I struggled to find funding for the concept. People with money thought Dr. Lisa on the Street was a nice gesture but weren't willing to write checks to support it. I thought, "This is going to be harder than I thought." As I became consumed by my pro-fessional clinical and leadership duties, I put Dr. Lisa on the Street on the back burner and invested my energy into com-munity outreach and my healthcare leadership work. In the back of my mind, however, I continued to think about how to bring more Dr. Lisa on the Street to the world. And in 2019, when I officially launched Grapevine Health, Dr. Lisa on the Street would be a cornerstone of the company.

During this period of time that I was not filming as much, my passion for plain language communication in healthcare never subsided. It emerged every time I saw a new patient frustrated by a confusing diagnosis, community members frightfully whispering in my ear about a symptom or a friend texting me about a confusing symptom or conversation with a doctor. Listening became my superpower. I became obsessed with understanding the kind of care and support people needed and why they were not getting it. I attended events to introduce myself to the community and volunteered at community organizations to hear what people were talking about and to answer health-related questions. I received so many questions about how the body "works," and so I bought an organ model. Many people learn visually, so I knew this could be a compelling aid to ensure the information I was delivering was more personalized and relatable. An executive at a local women's shelter invited me to engage with the residents. I carted my organ model into the facility, introduced myself and immediately opened the floor for questions.

The first question I received was, "How do people survive heart attacks?" I asked her to elaborate.

She said, "I heard when you have a heart attack your heart explodes. It doesn't sound like you should be able to survive an explosion in your chest."

I removed the heart from the model and identified the blood vessels, which enabled me to help her understand what happens in the body during a heart attack. Even now when people see me out in the community or watch the newer Dr. Lisa on the Street videos I have made since starting Grapevine Health, they know me because I am carrying my organ model which is an invitation to initiate conversations and educate about health information and misinformation.

During a clinical visit a patient told me she heard herpes turns into HIV. When I asked for more detail, it was clear she had somehow heard the statistic that people with ulcerating sexually transmitted infections have a higher likelihood of contracting HIV. On the grapevine among someone who doesn't understand disease pathophysiology or the why and how disease emerges, this might sound like herpes turns into HIV.

During the pandemic, I encountered many examples of health messages gone wrong on the grapevine. On a COVID-19 webinar question-and-answer session, someone asked me, "If my COVID-19 test was negative, why do I need to get vaccinated?" The pandemic experience is rife with examples illustrating why health literacy and trusted messengers are critical to health behavior change. In 2021, a friend asked if he could connect me with a friend whose family refused COVID-19 vaccinations. I agreed to hold a discussion with his parents, grandparents, siblings and cousins. Some of the questions were predictable and common like, "What's in the vaccine?" "What are the side effects?" and, "Why bother getting a vaccine?" Before closing out the session, I asked if the information was helpful in improving their confidence in the vaccine, and someone said, "Yes because no one has explained the information the way you just did. I understood everything you said."

I knew nothing I said was factually or scientifically different than anything Dr. Fauci or any other scientist was saying on CNN or MSNBC. The difference was I used metaphors and took great care to explain how and why things are the way they are. I learned if people have basic information about how and why the body and medicine work the way they do, not only does that foundation build trust and credibility, but it helps people hear and understand concepts in a way they can absorb.

Plain Language is Humanity

For a few years I stepped away from clinical medicine to work on health policy but continued community engagement activities as time allowed. I didn't realize it then, but I was building and refining the skills and messages I would later use in implementing Grapevine Health. Although I was no longer filming Dr. Lisa on the Street, I was continuing the work of connecting with patients that would serve me down the road. Many companies say they want to connect with "the community" but they have not adequately spent the time and energy to listen, engage with people and develop deep knowledge about their needs and concerns. I have done this work. Listening to patients and focusing on health literacy and its impacts during this time period helped me better understand healthcare delivery needs and predictors of engagement in care. I heard people's stories about how medical jargon confused them and discouraged them from returning for care. Most of these stories were from men. Health literacy and provider communication are linked, yet providers often de-prioritize plain language communication. I was invited to be a keynote speaker for a medical school to discuss health literacy as a provider imperative, and one of the doctors said time pressures prohibited him from spending time answering questions.

"There just isn't enough time," he said.

Time is an indisputable barrier in addressing the needs of complex patients in a clinic visit, but I reminded him we are communicating with patients verbally and non-verbally from the moment we walk into the room and it is our responsibility to ensure the language and manner in which we choose to speak to people and address their concerns are relevant and resonate for the person in front of us. This means our explanations and communications will vary from patient to patient, which can be perceived as time-consuming.

My return to clinical practice was equally full of joy and sadness because I saw firsthand how patient–provider communication influenced patient interest and outcomes. I began practicing at two hospitals, an academic medical center and a smaller, safety net, community hospital in a DC neighborhood with the highest rates of poverty and health inequity. Everything I saw was a preventable illness—preventable through access and preventable through trusted health information. So many of my patients living with HIV were burdened by shame and depression because of their infection. In my clinical work, we built a suite of wrap-around services to support them, and this included behavioral health therapy, care navigation and social services support for things like housing and food vouchers. We also implemented a home visit program for people whom we had not seen in a while. It worked—for a time. Members of our team would visit pregnant mothers and people with physical disabilities in their homes. The results were not always positive. Once our team went to a woman's house, and as they were leaving the house they witnessed a drug deal that made them feel unsafe. Safety concerns were always the enemy of community engagement. Despite this, I knew staying connected to the community was essential to maintaining trust and influencing healthcare-related behaviors. Even now patient engagement is the Achilles heel for insurance companies, healthcare providers and hospitals. This is where Grapevine Health would eventually come into play. What many of these organizations fail to recognize is that patient engagement is not a desk sport. People will not pick up the phone, click on your text message or open your email if they don't trust you or believe you to have genuine concern for them and for their community's well-being. The challenge with making these efforts, whether educational or more intensive outreach, is that it is sometimes hard to know if anything is working to shift their mindset toward health behaviors and if so, what exactly about it was successful.

Sometimes, our efforts paid off. One day I was in the cafeteria, and one of the patients I had attempted to visit at home walked over to me and said, "Hey Dr. Fitzpatrick. My neighbors told me you came to my house looking for me. I wanted to say thank you and I came to the hospital today to make an appointment. When you came to my house it made me realize you all really care and I should care about myself as much as y'all care about me." I wanted to cry.

Our approach was unorthodox and non-judgmental. I had deputized each person on our team to be creative and do their part to keep people engaged with us. A man was diagnosed in our emergency room, but by the time our navigator went down to escort him to our clinic he had left the building. The navigator called him. He was tearful and struggling with his diagnosis. She could not convince him to come back, so she asked another person on the team to try. Eventually, everyone on the team spoke to him. He was so afraid and distraught by his diagnosis that he was losing interest in our outreach. A team member called me and said, "Dr. Fitz, everyone on the team has talked to him and he won't come in. Can you call him?" I called his cell phone and he answered. I introduced myself and asked if I could come and talk to him. He was outside walking on Martin Luther King Ave in Southeast DC. I asked him to stay there. I drove to him, parked my car and walked over to talk to him about HIV treatment. I answered all of his questions right there on the street, and he showed up at the clinic the next day.

Another patient was afraid to come to the clinic for fear of being seen but agreed to meet me at a restaurant. I explained HIV treatment over a cup of coffee, and from then on, he engaged in care.

I learned a lot about the importance of plain language in healthcare from my patients. One day, a woman who was a college graduate and business executive was referred to me by a colleague for evaluation for HIV. The woman arrived at every appointment dressed in a suit. We developed a rhythm, and she eventually became comfortable with taking medications. But I noticed she rarely asked questions. I had been seeing her for over a year when one day she asked, "So doctor, how long do I have to live?" Confused, I asked, "What do you mean?" She said, "Every time I come here you look at my numbers and tell me I am doing great. I think you are just telling me what I want to hear but I want to know how long I will live because I have AIDS."

I was stunned and embarrassed. Stunned because I had no idea she didn't understand our conversations from the day we met and embarrassed because I had probably never said the words, "If you take this medication, you are not going to die from AIDS." Inspired, I used my pen to advocate for the elimination of the term AIDS from our vocabulary in the US when talking to people about HIV, because for so many it signifies death.[35] She showed me she had so deeply internalized these messages and that I had failed to communicate in plain language about her treatment and help establish expectations about the infection.

Bad Communication is Bad Medicine

The other place I learned about the need for trusted health information was on hospital rounds. Language barriers between physicians and patients tend to be a taboo subject in healthcare, yet it can contribute to confusion and mistrust.

I oversaw the care of medical students and doctors in training—interns and residents. Some were stellar, others not so much. Repeatedly, I witnessed miscommunication and a failure to communicate health information from resident physicians to patients. This problem was exacerbated when the resident physician was not born, raised and trained in the US.

One day in the barbershop I overheard a man tell his barber how he struggled to communicate with his doctor. The man's first language was an African language. His doctor also spoke English as a second language. His observation was that in order to understand his doctor, he needed to translate twice. He laughed this off saying he understood about fifty percent of the doctor's instructions because first he needed to translate the doctor's English and then translate that English into his language. As I listened, I wondered how effective the communication was between them and, more importantly, how it was impacting his care.

As conversations about health equity escalate in the US, we must create mechanisms to collaboratively discuss taboo subjects like the patient–provider discordance in language and culture and what impact this may have on patient engagement and outcomes. A 2020 JAMA publication reported lower patient satisfaction scores in racially discordant patient–provider pairs.[36] In addition, a meta-analysis conducted to better elucidate the impact of language concordance or discordance between English-speaking providers and patients with limited English proficiency on health outcomes was inconclusive due to mixed findings.[37] However, data are needed to better characterize the impact of cultural discordance between providers and Black patients. Sometimes cultural backgrounds of patients and providers are so dissimilar that it impacts care and communication, and this should be explored to determine the strength of the association with poor health outcomes. I noticed this at the bedside frequently after asking a patient their history and hearing discordance between the patient's version and the student or resident's understanding of what was being communicated due to culture. The US has a melting pot of healthcare providers and trainees born and trained outside the US. It is unfair to expect them to understand unique cultures and nuances of patient populations without training. A resident from Southeast Asia whose first job in the US was as a physician for low-income Black patients at a safety net hospital told me he primarily learned about American culture through the movies. This is a stark example of why the health equity agenda should include culture training of some kind.

Sometimes, I'd encounter a resident who just didn't seem to care about effective provider communication. One day in the clinic, a resident had seen a patient and came to me to sign off on the visit. He explained the situation, and then together we went to see the patient. The patient was sitting quietly in the corner. As I approached him and said hello, he smiled and nodded his head. I asked the patient a question, but there was no response. He smiled at me. I asked another question. He smiled but said nothing. I turned to the resident and said, "This man does not speak English; how did you communicate with him and what language does he speak?" The resident said he spoke Vietnamese but that they were able to communicate. I asked him if he spoke Vietnamese and he said no. The resident had feigned the entire history and likely physical exam. I was disgusted and wondered how often this was happening among our students and doctors in training.

On another occasion, I got a call from a resident who wanted to discharge a patient. I answered and he said, "Dr. Fitzpatrick, we are sending this patient home today and the lab called saying she has yeast in her blood. We think it is a contaminant but wanted to run it by you and see if we should send her home on an antibiotic just in case." I was mortified. First, yeast in the blood should *never* be considered a contaminant, especially in someone with poor immune system function because they cannot effectively fight the infection. Second, when I went to visit the patient, she had problems with her mental status and I was concerned she had meningitis. Upon speaking to the resident who was culturally dissimilar from the patient, born, raised and educated outside the US, it was clear there was a grave communication gap between him and the patient. The resident had not recognized the change in her speech and communication patterns. I called him to visit the patient's bedside with me and asked him about her speech. He said, "She sounds the same to me." I knew this was not true because I knew the patient from a previous hospitalization.

I am also concerned about the training our medical students and residents receive, particularly those who are caring for underserved community members. I suspect many are unprepared to recognize and understand cultural nuances that influence a person's healthcare outcomes and their willingness to engage in care.

If we were to explore disparities in care at institutions across the country, I suspect we would find hundreds if not thousands of cases like this. It is one of the reasons I become frustrated nowadays when I hear conversations about a health equity focus on collecting data.[38] There is a mountain of data to substantiate the need for specific interventions to address health inequity at hospitals, clinics and insurance companies across the country. We need to spend the time and effort assessing the data we have. If we look, we will find valuable information and realize there is no need to create new sources of data to address longstanding health inequities.

When I share my experiences learning about health literacy and why it matters with business-minded, corporate people, they are often unimpressed with improving health literacy as a business idea. They first want to know how this type of outreach scales. This is part of the challenge with the business of healthcare. The pronouncements about whole-person care, value-based care and patient engagement are abundant, but there is little appetite for or understanding about what is needed upstream on the path to scale. Scale can easily become the enemy of innovation for underserved communities because the financial ecosystem is not built to support the needs of people with social challenges or drivers of health like health literacy.

In the rush to acquire the latest and greatest computer software, healthcare widgets and apps, somewhere along the way people forget healthcare should really be about people, prevention and wellness. Our priorities should lie in meeting the needs of our patients and their communities. We cannot prioritize these needs without including an intention and focus on health literacy, because it matters to them. It certainly should matter to us.

Part 2

The Birth and Evolution of Grapevine Health

The journey of a thousand miles begins with a single step.

Lao Tzu

Grapevine Health is a social impact, for-profit, patient engagement company that leverages trusted messengers to deliver tailored, culturally appropriate digital content to help people navigate their health. We provide curbside access to the community on their terms, using videos, social media and soon text messaging to encourage people to pursue preventive care and take an active role in managing their health. Working with insurance companies while engaging directly with people in their communities, we act as a bridge between members and their healthcare plans. It is our combination of qualitative analysis and direct discussion with patients that allows us to make such important interventions in the healthcare system, especially for Medicaid enrollees and those who remain underserved.

DOI: 10.4324/9781003243502-2

Since graduating from medical school, every job and position I have held has proved relevant for this journey to help address the health information needs of the most vulnerable. In building, iterating and evolving Grapevine Health, I have learned through our engagements with patients, communities and customers that while improving health literacy is at the core of our mission, health literacy and health communication unavoidably intersect with many other drivers and predictors of healthcare engagement and outcomes. This path has required conversations and consideration about digital health innovation, social drivers of health, value-based care, HIPAA, healthcare delivery, healthcare financing and patient–provider relationships. This section shares the evolution of Grapevine Health from an idea which began as Dr. Lisa on the Street, to a unique and scalable patient engagement company that uses technology and direct engagement to address the foundational health information needs of underserved communities on their terms. The value of what we are building is clear. Health literacy and trusted health communication are vital players in the health ecosystems and are inextricably linked to everything we believe is required to address health inequity.

The Pivot

After the work I had done in clinical settings and in direct outreach, I decided it was time for a pivot. I applied for and was accepted into the Harvard Kennedy School of Government for a Master of Public Administration (MPA) so that I could learn how to take my background as a medical epidemiologist and infectious diseases doctor and apply it to social entrepreneurship and innovation. I wanted to make a larger difference and set my sights on Medicaid patients as the key community I was trying to reach. In 2015 I graduated from the Kennedy School as a budding entrepreneur, returned to Washington,

DC, and sent a message to Wayne Turnage, the head of DC Medicaid, asking if I could meet with him to discuss my ideas about patient engagement for the Medicaid program. He was gracious and appeared interested. He listened but I learned he was often deeply skeptical about the efficacy of ideas presented to him. The Medicaid program was not interested in my entrepreneurial ideas but had a Medical Director vacancy and instead offered me a job. Although I was still interested in starting a company focused on direct engagement and health literacy, I placed my entrepreneurial aspirations on hold, realizing the opportunity afforded me coveted access to and education about the inner workings of Medicaid.

Medicaid, like most health insurance, is a black box to providers and the public. It is overly complex, bureaucratic and governed by outdated legislation that can be disconnected from people's realities, thereby creating an unnecessary maze of activities to access care. What better way to learn and sift through the maze than to become part of it? What I cherished most about the experience was the opportunity to understand Medicaid patient utilization and also talk directly to patients and providers. When I called a doctor's office or organization and announced I was the Medical Director calling from the Medicaid program, people took my call, invited me to their offices and called me back. Even patients took my calls. Calling patients and identifying myself as Dr. Fitzpatrick from Medicaid invited people to complain about their services. Listening patiently to their concerns incurred goodwill, enabling me to ask the questions I had always wanted to know. Why had they used the emergency room (ER) instead of going to their doctor, or why had they chosen not to see a primary care doctor (PCP)? This nuance about *choosing* not to see primary care doctors is lost on many investors, startup companies and funders. The former suggests the person has an ongoing relationship with a doctor, and the latter suggests they have made a decision *not* to have a primary care doctor.

Many people I spoke to found the ER much more convenient and preferable than a relationship with a primary care provider. Understanding the nuance between having a PCP and choosing not to can influence strategy, business development and product design. From what I could tell, the venture capital and to an extent healthcare startup philosophies were built on decades of faulty information about cost drivers and people's interests in and motivation for interacting with the healthcare system. This makes it difficult to shift the perspectives and culture of those holding the purse.

During my tenure at Medicaid, the DC Department of Health commissioned a report by John Snow International to assess access to care barriers in Washington, DC.[39] I am often baffled by organizational leaders who choose to pay and believe findings delivered through consultants rather than through the experience and wisdom available within the organization. After working in the District at safety net hospitals for ten years, collaborating with community-based organizations and listening to people talk about their healthcare frustrations, I already knew we did not have a primary care access problem. Our problem was that people were not consistently using primary care and were instead in the ER and seeking sub-subspecialty care, which was much harder to access. The city had an engagement problem, which was the primary finding of the report.

I spoke to one of my primary care colleagues about whether or not she believed we had an engagement problem. She related a patient encounter that summed up part of the challenge. As she finished up the primary care visit, the patient stood up, gathered his things and said he was going to head over to the ER and get his foot checked out. Predictably she was taken aback and asked why he'd choose to go to the ER when he was right there with her in the clinic. He said, "If you take a look at it, you have to order an Xray and I will have to go to the hospital and get it; then it will take you a few days to get me the result and figure out what to do. If I go to the ER they can take care of all of that at one time." Some people see primary care as limited, lower value and less convenient. But from my calls I also knew there were other reasons people preferred the ER. The most common reason I call the one-night stand of healthcare.[40] No strings attached— "fix me, help me with *this* thing, right now, don't call me, I'll call you." The emergency department is convenient and always open. Now that people have smartphones, if they have a question or a problem, they will just as soon sit and watch their TV show or scroll on social media in the ER as sit and watch it at home. There are no co-pays for Medicaid so care is perceived as free. And there is no accountability to follow the medical advice given.

On the heels of the John Snow report I wanted to better understand the reasons for the lack of engagement in care and to understand if and how it was linked to health literacy. While I had learned a great deal by working from within the Medicaid system, I knew I needed the freedom to explore answers to these questions and to engage the community however I deemed appropriate, without the need to ask for permission. I knew I would have to leave the government to do this. It was a pivot I had been anticipating, but it was a hard decision because I was learning and engaged in so many meaningful initiatives.

I stayed in the Medicaid program for three and a half years, and it was a wonderful education. I learned about why insurance companies deny care and what the coverage determination process involves. I learned why it is so hard to change the way Medicaid does business. I learned that the program is not properly structured to keep people healthy. I learned that politicians are generally a barrier to getting people on a path to wellness. I learned most Medicaid programs are run by lawyers, policy and budget analysts and people who have never been part of a healthcare delivery system and, therefore, know very little about the clinical and social aspects of healthcare. Understanding Medicaid requires political savvy and a knack for interpreting and navigating regulations. Because of this, I knew staying in an administrative role would drive me further away from the problems I wanted to solve at the community level. Given the structure of Medicaid and the need for multi-layered and time-intensive approval to try things, I was compelled to embrace the pivot, leave the Medicaid program and become the entrepreneur I had initially set out to be when I'd completed my MPA at the Kennedy School.

Not Much Ado About Medicaid

After the experience I gained at Medicaid, I felt compelled to focus on health innovation for the poor and for people living in under-resourced communities. I had learned an astounding number of resources were being poured into health innovation, and almost none of it was being invested to design and optimize outcomes for Medicaid patients. The problems I was seeing and hearing about in the community were the basic bottom of the pyramid[41] needs and desires—a lack of human connection and support, unemployment, fear that stemmed from the inability to understand health information and reliance on hearsay as the most accessible and trusted health information source. At Medicaid, I had sat through countless company and startup pitches listening to founders discuss their solutions for dipping a toe in the Medicaid market. I never heard from a company exclusively serving and innovating for Medicaid. During my time at the Kennedy School, I interviewed several venture capitalists who felt investing in Medicaid was too risky and not amenable to significant returns on their investments. Those conversations came rushing back to me as these founders and companies all had the same refrain to explain why they were merely exploring Medicaid

rather than committing to it: "The margins are too thin."
Medicaid reimburses doctors less than Medicare, and Medicare
reimburses less than commercial insurance. They had been
indoctrinated in what I thought was somewhat of a false narrative, and the words were rolling off their tongues like they
were experts. Medicaid insurers are required to spend the
vast majority of their money on healthcare delivery, so compared to commercial insurance, there are fewer opportunities
to make money. State laws mandate how much plans must
spend on healthcare—the medical loss ratio or MLR—which
is up to eighty-five percent in some states.[42] This means their
profit margins are maxed at fifteen percent. If your budget
is five hundred million dollars, fifteen percent is significant
profit potential but apparently not significant enough to entice
investors and companies to prioritize Medicaid patients for
innovation. This is what companies mean when they say the
margins are "too thin." Since most insurance plans don't have
effective strategies to reduce avoidable costs, like emergency
room visits or hospitalizations, these costs eat into their potential profits. The theory is that the commercial insurers help
balance out the financing of the healthcare delivery ecosystem
because the money health systems and clinics can make on
commercially insured patients allows them to provide services
for more people on Medicaid or even those who are unin-
sured. It sounds like it should work, but it really doesn't work
all that well because commercially insured entities are not
crazy about the idea of providing care when they won't get
the same amount of money for people insured by government
sponsored insurance like Medicaid and Medicare.

I encountered this mindset a lot while working in safety
net hospitals. For example, a man with hepatitis showed up
in my clinic saying he had surgery at one of the more profitable hospital systems in DC and when they discharged him,
his only instructions were to follow up at my hospital. These
encounters pre-dated innovative digital information systems

that allowed me to see his medical history, so I had no idea what kind of surgery he had or why he had been hospitalized, and he could not tell me. Health systems will not admit they "dump" patients at safety net hospitals but that doesn't mean it is not happening. I heard about this on the street more times than I can count. Where is the humanity in dumping?

As a clinician, it was frustrating to be disrespected by more profitable health systems that failed to offer the courtesy of a referral phone call or take the time to send the patient with a detailed history and care summary. But the real tragedy is in the treatment of patients who are even more disrespected and treated as cash conduits. Once the health system has extracted the highest insurance reimbursement dollar value from them, usually from hospital admissions, diagnostics and surgical procedures, the patients are sent to safety net health systems for follow-up. The health system has no accountability mechanisms in place to interrupt or penalize these behaviors; thus, it becomes invisible when looking at health system performance globally. Patients know how they were treated but often cannot articulate their experiences. These experiences lead to the distrust of healthcare and healthcare providers. Consequently, this distrust manifests as high clinic "no show" rates, low medication usage or non-adherence and delays in seeking healthcare when patients need it. These low usage and adherence rates among the Medicaid population plague insurance companies and health systems across the US.

Health and Digital Health in the Hood

After resigning from Medicaid, I started consulting and conducting outreach and qualitative data collection for Medicaid Managed Care Organizations (MCOs). I was talking face-to-face with Medicaid patients, and this was when I decided it was time to use my experience in medicine, social innovation,

Medicaid and community outreach to launch a digital health company. I had known going all the way back to my earliest days filming Dr. Lisa on the Street that there was a clear need for people to be able to access on-demand, trusted health information. Previously I had been uncertain about how to make this intervention. But by now, everyone I spoke to used a smartphone and I was accustomed to always using mine as well. I therefore saw an opportunity to join the digital health revolution on behalf of Medicaid patients.

I wrote a blog describing some of my findings from community outreach and these conversations.[43] This publication ultimately led to my first funding from the Commonwealth Fund, a prestigious, academic-oriented, research and health policy-focused think tank.[44] They wanted to better understand mobile device access for underserved communities. I proposed a study entitled: "Exploring the acceptability and use of digital technology to improve patient engagement and delivery of health information." It was a qualitative study among Black and Hispanic Medicaid patients to understand mobile device access and use. With approval from an Institutional Review Board (IRB), we recruited the majority of patients from the emergency department (ED) waiting room at a safety net hospital. I found two graduate students to assist me, and we spoke to over three hundred Medicaid patients about their access to smartphones, what they were doing with those devices and where they turned for trusted health information. We learned everyone had access to some kind of device, and many of them had iPhones. Many of the iPhones were refurbished and could be purchased for less than one hundred dollars. In the Spanish-speaking community, friends and family would sometimes combine resources and subscribe to a group plan that enabled access to iPhones with the highest level of service and bandwidth. Seniors had phones, but their interest in engaging with them varied. One woman said, "I don't really know how to use it but I can call in an emergency." Another woman of similar age schooled me on ingenious ways she used her phone like a computer. She didn't have a computer or Wi-Fi at home but said, "Well you can get Wi-Fi just about anywhere. All the libraries have Wi-Fi, and a lot of businesses like Starbucks will let you use their Wi-Fi." She was not bothered by her lack of access to broadband. She completed job and social service applications on her phone. She had video chatting apps, streaming apps and games. In fact, she cut our interview short because she needed to listen to a webinar on her phone. I learned that while we were obsessing about the digital divide,[45,46] people without broadband access were seeing this as a condition of being poor or under-resourced and were finding ways to work around it. She had no health-related apps on her phone. After talking to her I started asking people to show me their apps. Like her, almost no one had downloaded a health-related app. If health apps were there, it was because the phone came pre-populated with them and they remained unused. Only one person, a senior, had an app for an electronic health record portal on his phone.

There were other significant findings from our study. Although our overall goal was to learn about digital health, health information and mobile phone access, we realized our learnings had broad applicability for thinking about health equity and social determinants of health solutions. It was clear that addressing poor health outcomes for this group would mean deeply engaging where they spent most of their time— in their communities. It also supported my suspicion that without this proximity, the health sector would continue to be unsuccessful in engaging low-income communities.

For most people we spoke to, health and healthcare are situational and rarely top of mind, which means many of the solutions designed to address health inequities are missing the mark. For example, lack of childcare interfered with people's motivations, interests and time needed to engage in care and preventive services. A mother with diabetes told us her insurance company offered a gym membership, but when she got off work, she would need a sitter and did not have the energy to exercise.

We also learned about what captures and maintains people's attention. Nearly everyone discussed their affinity for social media, but no one could name a health-related channel they followed consistently or used as a go-to source for health information.

A few themes emerged from discussions about healthcare access and experiences. Many believed the healthcare system was not respectful of and often prejudiced and unfriendly toward the poor. They also perceived doctors to be non-attentive and too busy to hear concerns. One person told us the healthcare system should be avoided unless "you are dying." This view was most prevalent among thirty-five to seventy-year-old men. Nearly everyone recognized the ED as the least appropriate form of care, but they used it for convenience.

Overwhelmingly, people were interested in and open to accessing health information, healthcare and support via smartphones. Nearly every person we spoke to had a cell phone. Similarly to the woman who frequented the library for Zoom meetings, they used their phones to conduct business of some kind including making conference calls, handling financial transactions, completing job applications and surfing the web. Most participants had no consistent access to healthcare providers through text or email. This support was largely non-existent after hours and only a few had used nurse lines for medical advice. Of those who had, some discussed their distrust of the nurse lines associated with their insurance providers. They described experiences with nurse lines as judgmental and condescending. A few people mentioned that the nurses "talk down to you" and "are just trying to keep you from spending their money."

Their advice for attracting and sustaining attention to health and health information was to make it easily accessible, personally relevant and entertaining. We asked people to recall recent health-related messages they'd seen and only a few people could. There was discussion about the Ebola scare from four years previously and influenza, and two people mentioned Obamacare and advertisements for what the community called Obama phones.

We shared clips from Dr. Lisa on the Street,[47] and the majority felt this strategy would be an attention grabber if they were short and funny and included people they knew, but they said the videos should be embedded in an app on their phone.

Several people felt hopeless about the ability to change the way low-income people engage with healthcare, sharing things like, "It's just like this in the hood and it's always been like this."

People told us the healthcare system is daunting and too complex. One person said she would often Google information she saw on television programs like Gray's Anatomy to verify the information before adhering to it. We were also told about home remedies passed down from generation to generation. One of the Hispanic participants shared a story about being skeptical about her primary care doctor's treatment so she sourced a different medication from her town in Mexico, which she says cleared her health condition. She never returned to the doctor.

Most notably, we learned specific information about smartphone access. Most people subscribed to plans through discount carriers like Boost Mobile, Metro PCS, T-Mobile or Cricket. These plans had competitive rates, most of which included unlimited texting and Internet for less than fifty dollars a month.

Although Internet access at high speeds was not yet universally available, people were resourceful about accessing services when needed, including public libraries for Internet access. To access higher-speed networks, some took advantage of Friends and Family discount plans and shared financial responsibility for the service. We learned five people could enroll in such a plan for one hundred dollars a month or twenty dollars per person. This strategy is employed by some Hispanic users to an even greater degree. For example, a group of eleven shared a single Friends and Family plan for four hundred dollars a month.

People complained about the limited space on phones. This is because (a) cheaper phones generally have less memory and (b) phones were pre-populated with numerous apps that couldn't be deleted from phones.

Although phone access is nearly universal, at the time of the study there seemed to be ownership tiers related to the type of phone, level of engagement and plan. These were:

1. Flip phones with and without texting but no mobile phone Internet access.
2. Smartphones with unlimited texting and Internet but limited space, storage and speed.
3. Smartphones such as iPhones and the latest Androids such as Samsung and LG with unlimited talk, text and Internet using 3G and 4G speeds.

As described, many people in the 3G and 4G tiers acquired this access through discounted Friends and Family plans. Nearly everyone described buying new phones using monthly payment plans over two-year contract periods. Friends and Family plan options are an important resource and provide expanded access that might not otherwise be available.

The use of social media was surprisingly high. Although most people reported most commonly using only two or three apps, we learned a lot about how people engaged with mobile phones. The results were slightly different among Black people and Hispanic people.

Black: Instagram, Pandora, YouTube, Facebook, Dominoes, Checkers, Solitaire, Candy Crush, Cash App

Hispanic: WhatsApp, Facebook, YouTube, Instagram, Solitaire

The apps most commonly used at that time were Instagram, YouTube, Facebook and Pandora. Several people used game apps, most commonly Candy Crush, Dominoes, Solitaire and Checkers. For the Hispanic population, WhatsApp was a favorite. We also learned that, in addition to Zoom, people used Facebook chat for group chats.

Because we recruited most people in the ED, we learned a lot about why people go there to seek care. This was a great opportunity because we knew ED use among the Medicaid population was an eternal and costly pain point for Medicaid insurers.[48] Almost everyone we spoke to in the ED waiting room had a primary care provider but chose the ED over going to their doctor. We also asked people to tell us if they thought their condition was a true emergency. Many people understood their conditions were low acuity and were willing to wait for more urgent cases or true emergencies to be seen. What I found most interesting was that when asked how frequently they used the ED almost everyone said *this* was an exception, an isolated case and outside their normal health-care usage behavior. One woman told us, "I never use the ED but I have to go out of town tomorrow morning, so I needed to come and get checked." Most people offered explanations like, "I don't usually go to the ER" and proceeded to discuss an extenuating circumstance that led them there. One person admitted to having a doctor and being able to secure an appointment but was unable to articulate why she chose the ED over waiting to see her doctor.

The most common explanations we heard for using the ED were:

1. The symptoms or need arose after hours.
2. Inability to secure an appointment in real time. Many were unwilling to wait twenty-four hours to see a doctor.

3. Medication refills. Some described challenges reaching their providers to obtain refills and knew these could be provided in the ED.
4. Reassurance. "I wanted to check just in case I needed medicine" was a common explanation.

As we collated and reviewed the data, our conclusion was that across the board, the healthcare system seemed to be building resources and tools underserved populations probably would not use, particularly if they were more outpatient clinics. Health care and prevention did not appear to be a high priority. People were often aware of resources and programs but didn't seem to have the energy or interest to engage with them. Actually, I could relate. It can take a lot of energy and motivation to engage even if it is for your benefit. I often procrastinate, so I understand what it is like to put something off for a tomorrow that never comes.

Above all, most participants admitted health was not on their day-to-day radar and that they would not actively seek preventive healthcare unless the issue was debilitating. One man said—as he smoked a joint—that he knows what he should do but rarely thought much about his own health. He jokingly said, "I would have to be dying before I go to a hospital." We also heard, particularly among men, that denial is a factor and that people disengage from care because they don't want to hear bad news or don't want to know about illness. Another man shared, "People do not act rationally when it comes to health. They may know what they should do but won't face it. I hate going to the doctor but I know I should." I could not disagree with him.

We also noticed a tendency for people to depersonalize issues or discuss what they heard or knew about someone else rather than personalizing their own experiences. For example, when discussing why people use the ED for non-emergencies, despite being recruited in the ED, many people offered an excuse for why their visit to the ED did not repre-sent a pattern but offered input about *others* who choose the ED over seeing a primary care doctor.

Most people used the Internet to query health information, but over fifty percent admitted their trusted sources of infor-mation were friends, family and people they knew. Few could trace the original source of the information but felt confident in its veracity because they heard it from someone they knew. Both Black and Hispanic populations described this same tendency toward word-of-mouth information sharing, what I referred to as the grapevine in Chapter One. This channel came across as much more powerful than traditional mecha-nisms of information delivery such as brochures, posters and branded media marketing.

Several people also described difficulty understanding provider instructions. The willingness to request clarifica-tion varied, including (a) saying nothing for fear of being perceived as ignorant, (b) asking a friend and (c) consulting the Internet. People perceived doctors were too busy to take time to respond to their questions or clarify explanations and information. Some also described a power imbalance between doctors and themselves, which was intimidating and discour-aged their engagement. One interviewee asked, "Are doctors even human?" as if to suggest providers are on a pedestal and different from them.

Above all, it appeared poverty was driving a lot of the disengagement we found. The wholistic view of people's environment, culture and personal challenges created a pow-erful narrative to help explain why engaging in healthcare was an afterthought for them. It is clear that living in low-income neighborhoods creates unique challenges that impact people's awareness of and ability to consistently engage in preventive and primary healthcare. For example, everything takes longer and many rely on public transportation, which subjects them to forces and timetables outside their control. Some trips to see a physician required transit on two buses and sometimes a train leading to more than an hour-long, one-way journey. A lot of insurance companies now offer ride-share benefits to offset these hassles, but if the primary care visit is not the priority, the benefit may go unused.

Our time in the community and the discussions we facilitated raised concerns about the emerging interest in social determinants of health. The need for healthier food, transportation, employment and housing services has long been recognized as a contributor to health inequities. But our interactions with the community through this project raised doubt about the ability of existing solutions to meaningfully impact the healthcare of low-income populations on a scale large enough to significantly address health inequity. This is because it appears engagement is being driven by urgency, and healthcare-seeking behavior is an exception rather than a rule.

It became clear to me that any efforts to dramatically shift the status quo would require a mechanism that places health messaging, services and resources squarely in the daily routine of members of this community.

Harnessing the Grapevine

After the study, we continued to deepen our connections to the community through outreach and partnerships with organizations. Mostly we were listening. We secured a Google number and offered it to community members to ask questions. The purpose was to see if anyone would use it and the types of questions they would ask. But we didn't have the budget to market the number and received only a handful of questions.

It was clear I would need to raise money to continue the mission and deploy a digital tool. After doing some research and interviewing a few tech developers, I knew I was in trouble. I did not have the resources.

Yet I did not want to stop this work even after the Commonwealth funding was completed. I decided I needed to deepen my understanding of the challenges to engagement and the use of digital tools among Medicaid patients. Given the small sample we had recruited, to generalize our findings and design a digital intervention would require a much more expansive effort. I wanted to design a collaborative study with a Medicaid MCO to better understand the nuances of digital engagement and what solutions would be appropriate.

First, however, I needed to formalize what my company was going to be and how we would make a meaningful impact on healthcare literacy and information access for Medicaid users.

When I reflected on the work I had completed through the Commonwealth Fund, what struck me was how the most rewarding aspect of the research engagement was the incidental storytelling. During discussion groups, people talked about their healthcare experiences and wanted to help others avoid the pitfalls they encountered. For example, an interviewee discussed his experience with a stroke. After recovery he began to understand how his lifestyle placed him at risk for stroke. He said he believed others could avoid having a stroke if they heard his story. There were also many discussions about bad healthcare experiences and negative interactions with hospitals, clinics, doctors and other members of the healthcare team. *This* was the power of the grapevine. Over half the participants told us their most trusted source of health information was friends and family. I realized that while the grapevine could frequently be used to spread misinformation, it could also be harnessed to spread positive, motivational and truthful information as well.

In the Black community there is a long legacy of passing trusted information on through the grapevine. Harriet Tubman led over three hundred slaves to freedom by communicating via the grapevine.[49] The civil rights movement was largely powered by the grapevine. And today, people informally share health information and recommendations on the grapevine. In Black communities a common source of information is "they." As in, "You know *they* say you should avoid that hospital." Or "*They* say those pills are poison." Or "*They* say, doctors ain't nothin' but drug dealers." "They" doesn't exist but rather is a proxy, a shorthand, for information flowing from block to block, bus stop to bus stop and barbershop to beauty shop. This information is informally transmitted at kitchen tables, corner stores, churches and even in the clinic waiting rooms.

As a result of this realization and our research study, my company now had a name: Grapevine Health. I wanted Grapevine Health to become a resource for community members to share a healthcare story or challenge they had overcome, thereby becoming trusted messengers for their neighbors, just as I had. But how could this trusted resource be leveraged to deliver health information at scale and improve outcomes? To answer that, I knew I needed to get proximal.

Learning from Proximity

Getting proximal enough to understand the impact of the Commonwealth findings, health literacy and its manifestations meant I had to listen and observe people even more in their environments. I am often consulted by people working inside four walls about how to reach underserved communities they deem hard to reach. I decided no one is hard to reach if I would humble myself and be "inconvenienced" enough to go to where people are, ask them questions and listen to the answers. Initially, my way of getting proximal was through service.

One of my first community engagements was volunteering at a men's shelter. It took a few weeks before the men began to talk. One man explained they wanted to first make sure I was going to stick around. Eventually, I routinely asked them to show and talk to me about their phones. The responses were similar to the people we engaged during the Commonwealth Fund study. The men were creative and resourceful about getting access to the Internet. Cell phones had become a lifeline for people in underserved communities, and the people I was talking to in health innovation, technology and business worlds did not seem to be aware of this. We needed to create mechanisms to establish digital communication with them and see what we could learn.

One day I was walking and passed a homeless man standing on the corner. He was staring at his phone and laughing hysterically. I stopped, greeted him and asked, "So what's so funny?" He turned the screen so I could see and said, "I'm watching *The Jeffersons* on YouTube." His phone was basic with a few apps pre-populated and mostly unused, but he was on the Internet watching videos and enjoying himself. I walked away marveling but frustrated by how far behind healthcare is in reaching people. It is as if we do the minimum needed to clear regulatory hurdles and avoid litigation and little else. Common mantras like "meeting people where they are," recognizing that "eighty percent of your health is related to non-clinical interventions" and "advancing health equity" appear in documents and are passionately espoused at podiums, meetings and in documents, but when I walk the streets and meet people like the man watching YouTube on his smartphone, it feels like these are just politically correct words devoid of meaningful and impactful action. As I thought about him, I knew the solution for improving health outcomes for the underserved had to incorporate digital solutions. While digital engagement is not a panacea, phones can be utilized as tools to build trust, educate and influence engagement in healthcare.

Our Commonwealth study findings kept playing out in the community. Almost everyone I encountered sought trusted health information from Google and to a lesser degree healthcare providers, but the sources they were most influenced by were the experiences and opinions of people they knew. In a moment of fear and need, people do the best they can to source information and obtain opinions about their health and healthcare and often that is through outreach to a familiar person with a shared identity. I once received a text message from a friend asking me what might be causing boils on his cousin's body. He asked me to text his cousin because the cousin did not like doctors but would be willing to talk to me because of my connection to him.

These requests for informal opinions and information also happen on the street. One day, a woman walked up and asked if she could get my opinion. She said her doctor was recommending she have surgery, but she was not sure if she could trust him and wanted to know if I thought it was necessary. That happened in DC. But the same thing happened in Philadelphia, Pennsylvania; Mobile, Alabama; Baton Rouge, Louisiana; Savannah, Georgia and Newark, New Jersey. There is a trust deficit in healthcare, and people crave access to someone they believe will tell them the truth. In the Black community, this is often a Black messenger.

Many of the stories I hear about how people are treated by healthcare institutions make me feel like a failure on behalf of the US health system. Miraculous things happen in healthcare every day. I am in awe of medical advancements and what we can accomplish with science, ingenuity and resources. The problem is that access to these miracles and innovations is so uneven that they are never top of mind for people when I am on the street or talking to Medicaid patients. Too many people feel left behind and forgotten. Too often, I hear, "They just don't care about us." But having worked across the health system and in august institutions, I know this is not the whole story.

A New Zip Code

By the time I started Grapevine Health, I had been listening, observing and studying people for decades. I would watch people everywhere. I could blend in Black neighborhoods and go pretty much unnoticed by others. On public transit, in grocery stores, open spaces and parks when I might appear to be in my own world, I was all the while observing. My superpowers are curiosity and listening, and my favorite questions are "how?" and "why?". In 2018, this curiosity led me to a personal pivot. I changed my zip code. To me, this was ultimately the only way I could get proximal enough to live and experience the challenges standing in the way of healthier communities. So I moved to one of the most underserved zip codes in DC. While the transition appeared sudden, I didn't make the decision overnight. The urgency to better understand drivers of poor engagement and outcomes had been building over decades.

Mortified by the obscene amount of money we spend on healthcare with such embarrassingly poor outcomes, I knew we must be missing something and that we could do better— I could do better. The US Medicaid program spends over seven hundred billion dollars annually on healthcare,[50] yet the health outcomes are largely unchanged. And in DC alone, the Medicaid budget is 3.1 billion dollars annually,[51] but despite a wealth of primary care access, the nation's capital has some of the worst health disparities in the country. In DC Black people are six times more likely to die from diabetes complications and twice as likely to die from heart disease as white people.[52] Georgetown University and my zip code are six miles apart, but people living in Georgetown live up to twenty-five years longer than the average person living in my zip code.[53,54] I wanted to understand why. The urgency to understand how a resource-rich city like DC could consistently, year after year, report about profound health disparities compelled me to become embedded in a community. It is a community where it can feel like time stands still. It is a community where, compared to wealthier parts of the city, few people vote or have income-earning potential to amass the tax revenue needed to become a priority for the city.[55] It is a community where people with low expectations for support become numb, discouraged and feel forgotten.

As I began exploring ways to build Grapevine Health, I interviewed community stakeholders, attended community meetings and showed up anywhere I could be a fly on the wall. One day in a community meeting I raised my hand and made a suggestion. One of the community leaders responded, "Dr. Fitzpatrick, we appreciate you but frankly if you don't live in this community you don't understand." I took offense because I grew up and had been working in underserved communities most of my career, including opening and operating a clinic in her community. It didn't matter; I was still seen as an outsider. Southeast was very familiar to me. I had started a non-profit organization there, I had been working in a leadership role at the safety net hospital in Southeast for three years, and above all, I had already gained the trust of many of the community-based organizations serving people in the community. But working in a community is not the same as living in it. After a while, I realized she was right. There were some things I would never understand without living in the community. I knew I had a lot to learn and I was ready to take the leap.

A few months later I rented my downtown condo in a posh zip code and moved into the neighborhood I was serving. I moved into my new neighborhood with enthusiasm and resolve. I was determined to engage with my neighbors and, in every way possible, live how they lived.

But my transition was rocky, and moving into the neighborhood was a culture shock. Despite my intentions, it is embarrassing to admit I had a sense of entitlement and elitism.

During my first few months in my new zip code, I was easily frustrated by what I eventually came to accept as social norms. During the first few months I was acutely aware of and frustrated by jaywalking, litter, the smell of weed and the sound of gunshots. Although Southeast DC was rapidly gentrifying, it was home to the lowest student graduation rates and highest rates of health inequity, poverty and gun violence in the city.

When taking Metro, before leaving the house I realized I was negotiating what I needed to take with me as must-haves and nice-to-haves. I had never done that before and realized it was because I was concerned about the safety of walking to the Metro. If I got robbed, I didn't want to lose important things that would be inconvenient to replace. My heart sank. But this became a ritual every time I rode Metro.

During my first week living in Southeast, I had gone to dinner on Capitol Hill and decided to take the Circulator bus home. There was a bus stop near my house. A third of the way home, a group of teenagers got on the bus and were shouting at each other. The noise was deafening. I got off the bus at the next stop and called Uber.

My attitude about my new neighborhood carried on like this for a few weeks with waxing and waning frustration, anger, regret and honestly, at times, disgust. There seemed to be no community, and I could not understand how people could thrive in such a chaotic, loud and disorganized environment. My world felt unstable. Imagine what it is like living in 20032. You hear sirens constantly; when you hear gunshots, you wonder if it is someone you know; you can't walk alone in the park. In fact, I had started walking and biking on a nearby trail, and after three 20032 incumbent residents advised against it for safety reasons, I stopped walking. I thought biking might be the answer, but after hearing about a bike jacking a few blocks from my house, I stopped that too. But I knew financially I couldn't move again, and my tenant had signed a year's lease. I would have to find a way to make peace with my new environment. A few weeks later, I was jolted by an experience that changed my perspective and led me to embrace my neighborhood, my reason for being there and see it through a new lens.

One day I boarded the green line Metro at Congress Heights Station. When I got on the train, I first heard the music, loud hip hop blaring through a small boom box. I looked to my left and caught the gaze of a man I suspect was in his twenties, spitting sunflower seed shells on the floor. He'd clearly been at it for some time because he'd amassed a sprawling pile all around his seat. He was in conversation with four other men his age all laughing and talking loudly, some of whom had their feet on the seats beside and in front of them. They had commandeered an entire section of the train as if to dare anyone to take a seat nearby. I sat down. I was angry. I thought, "How can they be so rude? They don't care who they are disturbing!"

Frustrated, I decided I'd make a quick exit to change cars at the next station. I stood up to exit the train, and just then a little boy, who could not have been more than ten, entered the train alone and sat down. The sight of him paralyzed me. I stayed on the train and sat down not far from him. If he was going to be on the train, I would stay on the train and not leave him there alone. I looked at the men and over at him; he had pulled out his phone and started playing a game. He had not once looked in their direction. He played on his phone completely unfazed by the commotion. It was as if he couldn't hear it. It hit me. He had become desensitized to the chaos. That day awakened me to the impact of trauma in a neighborhood. Not trauma inflicted by armed robbery, carjacking and gun violence, but subtle, chronic trauma persistently rumbling beneath the surface. It is so subtle it becomes unnoticeable. That is what I was witnessing with the little boy on the train. The chaos on the train was jarring for me because I had not yet become desensitized to it, but for him it was likely normal and part of the rhythm of the community, like breathing. That is the moment my perspective shifted about my neighborhood. In the past, if I encountered situations like this, because I had the ability and means, I would remove myself from the situation. He didn't have this option. And neither did over one hundred thousand people living in 20032 and adjacent and similar neighborhoods.

Fascinated and then sad, I thought about all the trauma a kid living in my neighborhood must endure and tuck away. And there it was. The answer to my question about the less obvious factors we are missing when analyzing the causes of health disparities and health inequity. Subtle trauma stirs up low levels of adrenaline and cortisol, hormones that contribute to systemic inflammation, which is the basis of nearly all if not all chronic health conditions.[56] This has been documented and is known as weathering among pregnant women.[57] The lack of safe spaces and inadequate access to or affordability of wholesome foods needed to support a body battled by constant and subtle trauma exacerbates the physiological response to trauma, which leads to chronic diseases. There is a large body of work by pediatricians highlighting adverse childhood experiences (ACES) and how the trauma associated with these experiences in childhood later manifests as they age into adulthood.[58] Despite the awareness, we have not created a national effort to address these problems.

Once I shifted my mindset and committed to staying, it did not take long to acculturate to my new environment. After living in Southeast for a year, I barely noticed litter, sirens, jaywalking and the sound of gunshots. I can also now distinguish the sound of gunfire from firecrackers. Subtle trauma is embedded in the rhythm of underserved communities, and over time, it becomes part of you. Eventually you just dance and dodge right along with it. That is what happened to me.

I knew I was fully embedded in community trauma when one day while talking to a colleague via Zoom, he stopped mid-sentence and asked, "Was that gunshots, Dr. Lisa?" I hadn't heard it. I would later realize my body was adapting to the subtle traumas and slowly transforming my health, in a negative way.

Despite the drama, riding Metro was a great way for me to observe community behavior. One day when riding the train, I noticed how the demographics of the people on the train shifted based on the Metro stop. These shifts revealed just how racially divided the city was. I took the train from U Street to Anacostia, and all the white people had left the train by the time we got to Navy Yard, which is a recently gentrified area. As we traveled to Anacostia, every face on the train was Black or brown. Yet nearly everyone on the train, no matter their stop, was always looking down, staring at a device. People are mesmerized by their phones. Some days I would walk up and down the cars scoping out what folks were doing or looking at on the phones—YouTube, Facebook, Instagram, Pandora, Spotify, Candy Crush, Words with Friends, Solitaire, the Bible. They were passing the time just like the folks who had participated in our study. Occasionally I asked people if they were using the paid version of these games and distractions. No one was paying, which meant there was an opportunity for Grapevine Health to capture their attention. I started playing word games on my phone to see what messages would pop up. I was amazed at how irrelevant they were. During the pandemic, the ads got better and told me how to find vaccines. But I was a bit annoyed that with all the information the health department and keepers of these ads had about me, they did not realize I had already been vaccinated so their ads were a waste of space. These observations endorsed my vision for pursuing digital health solutions for the underserved and helped transform how I thought about Grapevine Health and how we might deliver digital content to these communities.

Learning My Neighborhood

I was determined to engage with my neighbors in every way possible. I wanted to try to live how they lived. This meant riding public transportation, shopping in the neighborhood grocery store and exercising and biking in local parks. One of my first realizations after moving to 20032 was that I needed to buy a car. It was easy to live in downtown DC without a car because my world was in a one- to two-mile radius with everything I needed at my fingertips. I could walk, bike or take a short Lyft or Uber ride. Southeast was a different story. The place is spread out, and the main thoroughfares and intersections are congested, which means traveling three miles might take twice as long as traveling the same distance downtown. Once I wanted to travel from a community health center to the neighborhood hospital, a 3.1-mile journey, which is twelve minutes in a car but since the center was along a major bus thoroughfare, I decided the bus might be just as easy. Traveling 3.1 miles to the hospital took me just over one hour because I needed to transfer buses at the Metro station. Public transportation is a necessary service but reliance on it demands planning and time. It was another example of the glaring social disparities confronting my neighbors and me. When you are poor, time is a luxury and you are at the mercy of many things beyond your control. We often wonder why people skip clinic appointments. At times, waiting for public transportation thwarts the best-laid plans. I once encountered a young woman who asked for my advice on finding a new doctor. She relied on public transportation; the bus was thirty minutes late, and therefore so was she for her appointment. When she arrived, despite her explanations, the front desk attendant informed her she needed to reschedule because they had a ten-minute grace period. Nowadays, challenges like this have been slightly mitigated by access to ride-share benefits for transportation to clinic appointments.[59] But her experience highlights a greater opportunity for healthcare institutions committed to providing patient-centered care. Patients wait for doctors sometimes for hours, yet when physicians run late most are unlikely to extend the mutual courtesy. Similarly to the young woman, a senior shared her frustration with an ophthalmology appointment for her husband. The doctor was three and a half hours late for his clinic appointment. Incredulous, I asked, "Why didn't you leave?"

She said, "Because he needs to see! What choice did I have?"

She also felt trapped in the situation because it had taken several months to find an eye doctor who accepted his insurance. I knew from my time at Medicaid that there was an abundance of primary care options in Southeast, but that was not the problem. The greatest healthcare access challenges were with securing appointments with subspecialists because there were very few in Southeast, which meant traveling thirty minutes to an hour and a half across town to one of the hospitals. None of this was a surprise to me. One of the greatest lessons I learned was about how the social environment influences one's ability, willingness and interest to engage in healthcare. When your social environment is so complicated, inconvenient and time-consuming, it erodes your interest in preventive care or anything health related, unless, as I'd heard one man say, "I am dying." His health was only on his radar when it kept him from doing things he wanted to do. I began to understand.

My neighborhood was classified as a food desert.[60] I learned many of my neighbors didn't like the term, and those who had never heard it didn't believe it applied to them. My neighbor told me, "No one wants to live somewhere associated with being deserted. Plus, we are not in a desert."

Part of my sleuthing also included attending community meetings. I could figure out how to either get invited or show up in just about any space, listen, gather information and decide if I wanted to be seen or unseen. For example, I could go to food policy meetings or meet with food programs to understand their services and then take that understanding as I stood in line at the grocery store or corner store in my neighborhood to see if the rhetoric matched the reality. At one of these community meetings, a representative from the health department was boasting about the corner store initiative that supported the availability of fruits and vegetables at these establishments. Over the following week, I visited four of them, and while they all had fruits and vegetables, they were either on their way to spoiling or scant. At two of the stores I asked the clerk if people buy the produce and was told that most of the time, it rots and has to be replaced.

At city council meetings over the years, there have been a lot of discussions about subsidizing grocery stores in under-served communities. Council members would grandstand about the need to improve food access and in private people representing food retailers would share details about why their efforts had failed. One man said, "We tried and they robbed us blind. We couldn't make any money and the math didn't work." I noticed community members advocating for services would dismiss claims like this by saying the community is not at fault and the government needs to do more to incentivize retailers. The truth is in the middle. Safety and theft are concerning for retailers, but I really saw little honest and comprehensive dialogue about how a compromise could be achieved and what that might look like. More than a few times, I saw people stealing in my neighborhood grocery store. I also got scammed by a woman who meekly asked me to buy Depends. When we got to the register, the cashier said, "Are you buying these for her? Let me give you the receipt because if I don't, she will come back with it and get the money." I wasn't mad. I was impressed. Some of these scams are clever, conceived by brilliant but desperate people. Living in this neighborhood has taught me health inequity and poor health outcomes are largely driven by one thing. Poverty. And it's poverty that begets the trauma, PTSD, violence, low literacy, hunger and desperation so rife within underserved communities. I could see, if we were going to meaningfully improve people's overall state of health and well-being, we would have to address these too.

The Expense of Time and Poverty

Community conversations also helped me understand *why* people delay or avoid care. There isn't a single answer but a few themes. First, poverty as a driver of poor healthcare engagement is real. A friend once called me and asked if I would speak to a relative about a problem he was having with his shoulder. I accepted the call thinking the injury had just occurred. It turns out he was a construction worker and he had injured his shoulder three months before our call. I asked why he did not get it checked when he injured it and he said, "If I don't work, I don't get paid. If I don't get paid, my family won't eat." Oftentimes, people believe their symptoms will resolve spontaneously with time and are unable to discern when a symptom is grave enough to warrant attention. Second, seeking healthcare is perceived as inconvenient and time-consuming. "I don't have time to be sick" is a common explanation. The irony is that making time to engage in preventive behaviors avoids time lost long term, but the immediacy of a need clouds the ability to think about or prioritize the future. Third, people may not understand the role or value of primary care. Similarly to my colleague whose patient planned to leave her and go to the ER, I have called patients to ask why they missed clinic appointments and been told, "I was sick." Others have had trouble finding childcare, but ultimately, I believe, if we were providing a service seen as valuable and meaningful, people would come. The challenge is ours to understand and address these perceptions.

The notion that health outcomes and disparities are linked to poverty and social environments is not a revelation. Social epidemiologists and social science researchers have been high-lighting these associations for decades. I believe our failure to act on poverty stems from two realities: (1) it feels overwhelming to address poverty and (2) we do not have the will to address it because of the power shifts it will create in society.

With wealth comes agency or the ability to act and think with self-determination. I remember watching Michael Moore's movie *Sicko* many years ago and being struck by comments from Tony Benn, a former British Member of Parliament. In response to Moore's question about choice and freedom to choose, he says,

> Choice depends on freedom to choose and if you are shackled with debt, you don't have the freedom to choose. People in debt become hopeless and hopeless people don't vote. If the poor turned out and voted for people who represented their interests it would be a real democratic revolution. Keeping people hopeless and pessimistic. People are con-trolled by [fear and demoralization]. An educated, healthy and confident nation is harder to govern and politicians don't want that because they would get out of control. One percent own eighty percent of the world's wealth and people put up with it because they are poor, demoralized and frightened so they think the safest thing to do is take orders and hope for the best.[61]

This is the best description I have seen describing the social and financial shackles imposed on people that prohibit them from prioritizing their health and wellbeing.

At the Centers for Disease Control and Prevention (CDC), when our investigation assessing root causes of HIV transmission among Black women highlighted poverty as a driver of HIV disparities, the leadership's response was, "We don't do poverty." Wealth disparities drive health inequity, and we don't need more data to characterize this problem. We need the will to address it.

Doctors are Drug Dealers

One of the most common themes I heard in the community was that doctors are untrustworthy because they are drug dealers. This perception is another factor that leads people to avoid or delay care. For a long time it was uncomfortable to hear this repeatedly. I heard it on the street, in one-on-one conversations and at community meetings. The comment was often preceded by statements like, "No offense…" or, "Not you, but…." When I started probing and listening openly, the comment made sense and now I understand why people believe this. It is related to health literacy as a driver of healthcare engagement and health outcomes. As doctors, we are failing to build trust through communication. We are failing to educate patients and the community in a way they can understand. We are failing to address health literacy. We take for granted what people know about their bodies, healthcare, how insurance works, nutrition and so much more. I understand why people believe doctors are drug dealers because in a setting of poor health communication, it becomes about optics and people are left to draw their own conclusions. While consulting for an insurance company, I interviewed a man who was recently diagnosed with diabetes during a hospitalization. He was the first person to reorient my thinking about doctors as drug dealers. In our conversation, he used the phrase and I said, "Tell me about that. Why do you think doctors are drug dealers?"

"Because no matter what is wrong with you, all they want to do is write you a bunch of prescriptions."

"Is that what happened to you?"

"Yes. So, for instance, I was having headaches and they got so bad I thought let me just go there and see what the doctor thinks."

"OK."

"So, I tell him about my headache and he starts asking all these questions that had nothing to do with my headache. And then he started poking and prodding me everywhere except my head. It's like he was looking for something he could write a pill for. And sure enough before I left there he told me I had high blood pressure and diabetes and I walked out of there with three prescriptions and wasn't none of them for my headache. I'm telling you the doctors are working for the drug companies. They might wear white coats but they ain't nothing but a bunch of drug dealers."

I was nodding and understood completely. It was crystal clear.

Humbly, I asked, "Can I tell you what I heard in your story?"

"Sure."

"A lot of times doctors don't take the time to explain why we do things. There is a reason the doctor asked you all those questions. It is because anytime a person has a headache that is a signal that something is going on somewhere in your body and it may not necessarily be in your head. A lot of times people think headache means brain cancer or something wrong with your brain but most of the time, the headache is showing up because something else is going wrong and a lot times, especially in our community, that is because the person has high blood pressure. We ask all those questions because we are trying to figure out what is causing the headache. Does that make sense?"

"Well yeah but he didn't explain it like that. That's all he had to say."

"So, what was your blood pressure when you went in?"

"I don't remember, he told me to start writing it down. But I remember the number on the bottom was over a hundred."

"That is high blood pressure and high blood pressure causes strokes."

"Then he could have just said that."

Of course, I don't know what transpired in that visit but I suspect the doctor made this connection but communicated it in unintelligible language so the man left frustrated because he got prescriptions but still had a headache. This is one of the best examples I have encountered about how poor communication between doctors and patients is dangerous and severely erodes trust in the relationship.

The Power of Trust

By the time I moved to Southeast I had talked to thousands of people about health, health information and engagement in healthcare. When it came to understanding engagement in healthcare, no single issue surfaced more than trust. Washington, DC, has one of the nation's richest and most generous Medicaid programs and enables access to care for the poor, which means that combined with all other insurance types, the District has insured over ninety six percent of its residents.[62] The primary care safety net is vast, with at least nine Federally Qualified Health Centers and dozens of primary care offices scattered across the city.[63] Between high insurance coverage and abundant primary care access, I wanted to understand why people in my neighborhood were less likely to keep clinic appointments. I started asking my neighbors.

One of my neighbors proved to be my best source of learning and information. He was a small-framed, sixty-something Black man with a playful sense of humor and a tendency to wander around the neighborhood. He was a popular opinion leader on the block and seemed to know everyone's business and the latest social developments in the neighborhood. When I wanted to get the scoop, I called or looked for him. One day we walked to Metro together, and he told me he was going to a doctor's appointment. That conversation opened the door for me to freely inquire about his health and ask follow-up questions. Listening to him talk was like playing a highlights reel from all the conversations I'd had with patients and the community over the years. He had experienced and perceived all the bias, racism, skepticism and distrust conveyed to me. He talked about his distrust of doctors because he didn't understand what they were saying to him. He said, "Those doctors talk so fast and use those big words but they do that on purpose so they can pump you full of medicine so they can make money. It's all about the money for them." When I asked him if he takes his medication he said, "Sometimes. It depends on how I feel but most of the time I feel good and I really don't think I need that medicine." He told me about a pill he hardly takes because it makes him run to the bathroom. "I take Metro to my job and there ain't no bathroom on the Metro. So what? Do they want me to pee all over people on my way to work?" He chuckled. I also had trouble convincing him I was a doctor. I told him a few times, but it didn't register. One day I asked, "Why don't you believe I am a doctor? I really am." He said, "Because you are too nice to be a doctor. Doctors are usually up there on a pedestal talking down to you. And you talk to everybody."

His comment reminded me of an encounter a few blocks from where we were standing. I had lost my purse, and someone returned it to my house. My Ring camera picked up his image so I set out on foot to find him. On my walk I encountered a group of middle-aged to older men sitting in the alley. I walked over, said hello, showed them the picture and asked if anyone knew him. Someone asked, "What do you want with him? Are you a parole officer?" Another asked, "Are you a social worker?" I told them I was a doctor and started chatting with them. One of the men slowly moved away from the group and stood alone against the wall. After a few minutes, he shouted to the group, "Man, y'all better be careful. Don't trust her. Where did she come from? Why you asking so many questions? And she too friendly. She just too friendly!" I asked him if he wanted me to prove to him I was a doctor. He said yes, so I walked back home, retrieved my hospital badge, white coat and stethoscope and went back to the alley. I showed him and then pulled up my LinkedIn profile. He looked at it and yelled over, "Well I be damned y'all she really is a doctor." I asked why it was so hard for him to believe I was a doctor. He said, "Because you don't just see doctors walking around in *this* neighborhood." Another man apologized and said, "Well can you blame us? You don't ever see doctors walking around in the community and certainly not talking to us in the alley."

I had heard this before. In healthcare we talk a lot about being community centric, but if you ask the community what that means, it means we have to come out of our buildings, be on "equal" footing and engage with people in their environments. We have to show people that doctors are trustworthy and have their best interests at heart. How can we expect people to trust us and our expertise if we do not make this effort to talk, listen and engage?

Because of the dearth of Black doctors seen in the community, I have been asked to prove I was a doctor in other settings, too. The first time it happened during my residency in 1995, I was traveling back to the US from Africa through Heathrow Airport. A customs agent stopped me and searched my belongings, and when I told her I was a doctor she demanded documentation to prove it. The next time I remember it happening was in 2016 during my time as Medical Director at DC Medicaid. I rode my bike to meet with a community clinic director. When I got to the door a man was standing outside guarding the door and refused my entry. I said, "I am Dr. Fitzpatrick with the Medicaid program and I have a meeting with the clinic director." He didn't trust I was being truthful and asked me to prove I was a doctor. Once I was inside, he apologized profusely and went to grab two of his colleagues and brought them to see me. He said to his colleagues, "See, look. She's a doctor." He was a Black man who apparently had never encountered a Black doctor. I still find that hard to believe because we live in DC where Black professionals are abundant. But, clearly, in his community Black doctors are not visible enough.

When it came to deeply understanding and providing context about how distrust influences healthcare outcomes, medication adherence and engagement in healthcare, my neighbor was the gift that kept giving. I grew accustomed to seeing him a few times a week. One day I ran into him and realized it had been a few weeks since I had seen him. I asked where he'd been.

He said, "I been in the hospital. The doctors tried to tell me there is something wrong with my heart so they could keep me all pumped up on medicines and IVs. But there is nothing wrong with my heart."

He pumped his chest and said, "Look at me! I feel good!"

I said, "Well why did you bother going to the hospital in the first place?"

He said, "I couldn't breathe." I asked if anyone explained how his trouble breathing was related to his heart. He said they'd mentioned something about it, but he didn't catch it all because they were talking fast and using big words.

Standing there on the street corner, I told him about the connection between his heart and lungs and said that if his heart was not pumping blood well, fluid would get backed up in his body so they need to use medicines to help his heart pump and to get the extra water out of his body.

He said, "Well why didn't they just say that? They didn't explain it like that."

I asked if he was taking his medicine.

He said, "I might take it now and then but they keep changing my medicine and I get confused with all the pills."

He had not told them he was not taking the medication, so the doctors assumed what they prescribed was ineffective and kept adjusting his medications. A few months later, I saw him and he had a heart pump. I said, "I thought you said there was nothing wrong with your heart." He said, "I don't think there is but I said yes just in case. I will see how it does with this thing."

My neighbor and the way he processes his illnesses and thinks about doctors should be instructive for healthcare leaders, problem solvers and innovators. It is because of people like him I became more devoted than ever to building a solution to deliver trusted, relatable and understandable health information to my community.

Another neighbor, a sixty-something man with diabetes and a heart condition, told me he doesn't trust doctors and yet appears to be completely dependent on them. I saw him while out walking one day. I waved and crossed the street to chat. He told me he had been in the hospital. I asked what happened. He said, "Those doctors told me I have a heart problem but you see I am here standing in front of you. How can there be something wrong with my heart?" He reminded me of the guy with the headache. I asked, "How did you end up in the hospital?" He said, "I passed out."

I'd see him from time to time and he'd tell me how he still didn't trust his doctors because they kept giving him medicine because they needed money. I asked him what it would take to get him to trust doctors, and he said, "I don't know if I can but they can stop giving me all this medicine." I had also been trying to convince him that I am a doctor. He said he didn't believe I was a doctor because I was so nice and because I was always talking to people.

The greatest lesson I learned about community trust and connection happened during a street encounter. Our team had set up an information table on Good Hope Road in Southeast DC across from the 7-Eleven. For about an hour, I noticed a woman walking back and forth observing us. She'd stop and listen from a distance and then walk away. I saw her walking across the street from the 7-Eleven toward me. She had a banana in each hand, one of which she was eating. She walked over and gave me the other banana and said, "I bought this for you."

Genuinely touched, I thanked her and put the banana in my pocket. She said, "I want you to eat the banana."

I said, "I'm busy right now, but this is exactly the kind of banana I like, no spots and I will definitely eat it later."

She said, "I want to watch you eat it right now."

I said, "OK. Tell me why it is so important to you that I eat this banana right now, and I will take a bite."

She said, "I want to see if you trust us."

I was stunned. She was teaching me that trust is bi-directional. She was not impressed that I showed up on the street. That could just be for show. She wanted to know if I respected her from one human to another. She wanted to know if I saw her as my equal. She blew me away. I ate the entire banana and it was delicious.

I have told this story numerous times to people working across the sector, and most people I told were skeptical and hoped I had refused to eat the banana because they believed she meant me harm. But our perspectives are formed by our realities. I spend a lot of time on the street engaging with people. I have developed an intuition about human behavior, danger and safety. Because I was comfortable in that moment with her, it never occurred to me that she meant me harm.

This encounter with the banana lady made a deep impression on me as a servant leader. No matter our station in healthcare, whether provider, administrator, creator, helper or leader, we must approach our work with humility and, above all, humanity.

Medicaid and Sloppy Seconds

When I first began partnering with Medicaid MCOs to understand how best to engage people in preventive services and screenings, the qualitative data collection among Medicaid patients consistently showed that people insured by Medicaid often felt uncomfortable seeking healthcare. Once I interviewed a woman who was released from her job that had afforded her employer-based, commercial insurance and due to a disability was now enrolled in Medicaid. She said, "Medicaid is junk insurance and they give us sloppy seconds." She said she noticed differences in wait times to get an appointment, availability of providers and attitudes of front desk staff both in person and on the phone.

During the pandemic I would enroll in Medicaid myself while I had lost my income so that I could find out what the experience was like from the patient's perspective. I too found it difficult to navigate, with long wait times and even no response when I called. I was never able to schedule a primary care appointment because no one ever picked up. When I arrived at Washington Radiology for a mammogram, they told me they did not take Medicaid and said I could not pay for the procedure out of pocket. But when I returned after reinstating my commercial insurance, I was told it was my option to pay out of pocket if I preferred. From these experiences I certainly understood why Medicaid patients I talked to were often frustrated by the way they were treated when seeking care.

I have heard similar complaints from the homeless community. During an outreach event, I joined a community group distributing bags of food to the homeless people living in a park. As I helped stuff the Ziploc bags, I was embarrassed because I knew the food we were giving them was not appropriate. It was all processed foods with empty calories like snack cakes, chips and cookies. While out in the park, I tried to hand a bag to a gentleman and he cursed at me and said, "Why are you giving me that? Would you eat that? Would you put that junk in your body? Get away from me with that." I knew he was right. I felt ashamed. The last thing unstably housed people need is junk food. But this is the norm. Do we inflict more harm than good with our service events like this? I mentioned it to one of the other volunteers and he said, "They should be grateful someone is trying to help them." My heart sank. I did not agree. The encounter really bothered me. What are our motives for conducting outreach? Are we doing so for ourselves? Is our way of giving back meaningful and helping to put people on a path to stability and a healthy life? In medicine we talk a lot about doing no harm but I think it would behoove those in social support services to do the same and treat people as we would want to be treated.

Learning from the Homeless

As I was collecting data and discussing with Medicaid patients the reasons they do not engage in regular preventive healthcare, I realized I needed to better understand the homeless population and how to support their healthcare needs. This is another group of people deemed "hard to reach," but in the same way that doctors need to go out into the community to engage with people on their terms, we also need to connect with and understand the homeless if we want to provide better care and have them seek out and trust our services. I began volunteering at a men's shelter, and one year I joined a sleepout for homelessness to understand what it is like to sleep on the street. People often tell me to be careful when I describe my engagement with people who are homeless. It is as if people believe a person is inherently dangerous because they are unhoused. There are many biases and inappropriate, misguided stereotypes about homeless people. I have learned and been guided by their experiences and wisdom. For example, although there is an undeniable correlation between substance use disorders and homelessness,[64] many of the behaviors witnessed on the street are sometimes not from drug and alcohol use but rather are attributable simply to a lack of sleep. Access to safe, uninterrupted sleep is imperative for brain and physical function. I saw this repeatedly when interacting with many of the men in the shelter.

The stories they shared about their paths to homelessness highlighted how poor schools and education, lack of family support and guidance as well as easy access to addictive substances can limit opportunity and derail plans and desires for a different life. Their stories highlight why empathy rather than judgment is essential for engaging and improving health outcomes for people who are unhoused. They also remind me how powerful a story can be to educate and help understand how best to approach or help someone in need.

After serving lunch one day at the shelter, a man told me he lost his apartment because his landlord threatened to evict him if he didn't seek help for his addiction. The threat of eviction was hugely embarrassing for him so he packed up his belongings and started living on the street. His children lived nearby but he refused to burden them and said, "I was raised to stand on my own two feet."

I said, "But it's your family."

He insisted, "No, I have to provide for myself."

I said, "Are you too proud?"

He said, "It's not pride. I am a man and I have to handle my own business."

This conversation is reflective of many conversations I have had with male patients about their delays in seeking health support and healthcare. Believing their problems would spontaneously resolve or that seeking help is weakness, their health concerns often accelerate to life-threatening conditions. But I have learned a person cannot be forced to accept healthcare and even social support. Each person has to decide when and how to accept help. These encounters also helped me understand the moral imperative to employ non-traditional strategies to engage and support people from underserved communities on their terms. It is not appropriate and often does not help to push, force or expect people to conform to existing healthcare delivery standards and processes.

Lessons from working with homeless people inform any engagement we at Grapevine Health attempt with this population. First, smartphones are not a luxury but a survival tool and lifeline. Nearly everyone I have encountered has a smartphone. Often these smartphones are lost or stolen, which means it is critical to ensure knowledge about and access to on-demand support to obtain or replace them. There is a misconception about homeless people's ability to use technology. Similarly to my experience with the man on the corner laughing at *The Jeffersons*, it is myopic to believe one's income and even formal education dictate their ability to learn and use technology. The problem in healthcare and digital health specifically is a failure to deeply understand and incorporate the technology needs of underserved communities so that these insights can be leveraged to provide access and support.

Second, I learned even more than usual that trust must be earned over time and is never instantaneous with a stranger. While out on a morning walk with a friend I met a Spanish-speaking, elderly gentleman pushing a cart. I had seen him several mornings, so in my broken Spanish I asked him if he needed help with housing. He seemed open to the support. Since I had the phone number of the CEO of a social services agency on my phone, I called her and shared his location and first name so their outreach team could find him. As we walked away, my friend said, "You should take a picture so they can find him." I said, "That is a good idea." It was a momentary lapse in judgment. It was a terrible idea. But I went back to see if I could take his picture, and he immediately became belligerent and gestured to me to leave him alone. Of course an undocumented person with whom I couldn't adequately communicate didn't want me to take his picture. That was not a news flash. Despite my blunder, I suspect they found him because I never saw him again.

Similarly, I passed a woman on my walk who asked if I would buy her breakfast. I told her I would on my way back. By the time I returned, she had found someone else to buy her coffee and pastry. I asked if there were other ways I could help and she wanted to know what kind of support I was offering. She was interested until I started asking too many questions, including "Are you from DC?"—which seemed a harmless question because I was trying to understand if she could access DC services or those outside DC. My questions caused a shift in her tone and demeanor, and she completely shut down. I knew any attempts to further engage her right then would mean if I ever saw her again, I had no chance.

Finally, during a discussion group I was conducting at a men's shelter, I asked for thoughts about why people avoided doctors. Exasperated, a man shouted, "Because we don't understand what y'all are saying and if I can't understand what you are saying, I don't trust you." I have heard many versions of this comment throughout the community. Our failure to communicate medical information in plain language exacerbates distrust because it makes people feel as if we are hiding something and benefiting at their expense. Failure to communicate in plain language leads to fear, and fear leads to disengagement from care and support. Therefore, chief among our duties as healers, health coaches, advisors and helpers is to allay fears by explaining the health conditions we are diagnosing.

Grapevine Health is (Almost) Under Way

Making meaningful change in a community is never the work of one person. I knew from my efforts at Medicaid, with the Commonwealth Fund and filming as Dr. Lisa on the Street that if I wanted Grapevine Health to make a measurable difference in the community, I would need a team. And I knew who to contact. I first met Dr. Neal Sikka when I was working at Medicaid. Dr. Neal is an emergency physician and Associate Professor at George Washington University. He is also a telemedicine expert who had been trying to figure out why Medicaid wasn't using more technology to reach patients. This was similar to the questions I had been asking for almost a decade. What technology would best serve the Medicaid population? How could we use digital innovations to engage Medicaid members and encourage them to access primary care and healthcare services before preventable diseases worsened—or even before they began? Above all, how could we as doctors bring a community focus to our messaging that would improve health literacy and health outcomes among Black and brown populations in underserved communities?

Advised by a team of strategists and innovators, including Dr. Neal, I began securing the first contracts to fund Grapevine Health. We were especially looking to work with insurance companies and MCOs. These Medicaid managed care companies are private health plans that receive state funding to cover Medicaid costs. Most Medicaid beneficiaries are covered by MCOs, yet our qualitative research and our discussions in the community have shown time and time again that there are many reasons a majority of Medicaid members are not seeking preventive care services or managing both acute and chronic health conditions. Grapevine Health emerged as a company designed to bridge this gap between patients and their insurers, acting as a trusted messenger to deliver information, correct misinformation and answer people's questions in a clear and accessible way. With the success of the Commonwealth Fund study and confidence in our message and our work, by 2019 we were ready to officially launch Grapevine Health in DC. It would prove to be a challenging—and rewarding—time to get our message out.

And Then There Was a Pandemic

The COVID-19 pandemic turned out to be a crisis tailor made for the newly formed Grapevine Health. The world soon saw the need and understood the urgency for tailored, digitally accessible health information delivered by trusted messengers. In many cases it worked, which afforded us proof points and demonstrated the power of Grapevine Health and our trusted messenger approach. At first, however, we had to find our footing and, like the rest of the world, adapt to this new and changed reality.

Early Days

I first learned about SARS-CoV2 in November 2019. The reports about the Chinese ICU doctor who tried to warn the world about a new virus that was behaving atypically mostly went unheeded, including by me.

The first question I received about the pandemic was in early February 2020 from an Aspen Institute colleague. We were at dinner in Austin, Texas, with several others from our cohort in the Aspen Global Leadership Network.[65] "Should

I be worried about coronavirus?" he asked. My flippant and dismissive response reflected a combination of faith in CDC, knowledge of past SARS-related outbreaks in Asia and a woefully inadequate understanding of the nature of events unfolding overseas. "This will likely pass. I'd be more worried about the flu right now." It is humbling to reflect on that moment and recognize how uninformed and disinterested I was about events to come. Even when we learned about the first outbreaks in the Northwest,[66] I remained unmoved, believing CDC was on the case containing the spread. After all, this situation was tailor made for CDC's mission. The Centers for Disease Control and Prevention began as a malaria control unit and over the years had evolved to become the nation's leading public health authority, providing health guidance and mitigating the impact of public health threats in the US and to some extent around the world.[67] I was intimately familiar with the role of CDC, having been an Epidemic Intelligence Service Officer[68] and working at the agency for nearly ten years. I was confident that we were crying wolf. That is, until we learned CDC had bungled testing access. Case finding is fundamental to outbreak control, and if testing is not widely available and easily accessible, there is no way to contain the outbreak. I watched in disbelief as the news unfolded about how much time was lost in early case identification. Around this time, my phone started ringing and text messages started rolling in. "How do I know if I need a test?" "Where can I get a test?" "Are the tests accurate?" The news in New York City was not good as the death toll started rising.

Before the pandemic took hold in the US, Grapevine Health had three pending contracts from insurance companies eager for our on-the-ground, digitally based approach. As the news became graver and reality set in about the pandemic, all of these contracts were indefinitely placed on hold. We had no income coming in.

When the lockdowns were announced, I immediately worried about the underserved. Forgotten people who, on a good day, could access services only four to six weeks after a request and on a bad day were invisible. The lockdown slogan was #stayhome coupled with a national refrain, "We're all in this together," which rang out across the media, including on social media. I knew it wasn't true. I contacted CEO leaders of social services organizations in DC who I knew were providing services for people living in or near poverty. I wrote a blog in Forbes Health, "We Are Not All in This Together."[69] It did not take long for more people to realize that frontline workers could not stay home, and that people experiencing homelessness had no homes and thus felt isolated and alienated from the national moment of solidarity.

In early March before masks were endorsed as part of the national prevention strategy, I was curious to know how the policy shifts were affecting people, so I went outside; I was parroting CDC and telling people only those who had symptoms needed to wear masks. I encountered a group of people handing out food and went over to speak to a man I saw wearing a mask. I said, "You know you don't need to wear a mask unless you have symptoms." He grimaced. He had something to say but first wanted to ensure he had an audience. He shouted, "Hey listen up everybody. The doc said you are not supposed to wear the mask unless you have symptoms. So I said to doc, the spray can come out of the side of the mask. We've been talking—what if someone has those symptoms and is not wearing a mask. I am protecting myself." The grapevine was ablaze with advice about how to protect yourself from "The Rona." His comments and logic proved prescient, and once again, I was humbled by community wisdom and the fallibility of our knowledge. Next, I asked a young lady what she had heard about coronavirus and she said, "Only that it is killing us." Her impression was that the virus was preferentially affecting Black communities. I later learned she had already lost three people to COVID-19.

A few days later I decided to do a walkabout in one of the poorest and under-resourced zip codes in the District. I was wearing my white coat hoping to bolster my credibility and people's willingness to talk by signaling I was a doctor. It worked pretty well. I talked to over a dozen people on the street that day. Some weren't consuming news and were getting pandemic information solely through the grapevine. Others were watching social media and falling prey to myths about the virus like that it was fictional and a public emergency falsified by the DC government to pave the way to install 5G throughout communities that historically opposed their installation. I heard from people who asked where and how to get a COVID-19 test and a woman with asthma who pulled me away from the crowd to ask how she could differentiate her asthma symptoms from COVID-19. She had a young child and older parents at home and was concerned about their well-being. She also was concerned about how a COVID-19 diagnosis might affect her employment because she did not have sick leave and couldn't take off were she to test positive. As the news escalated and conflicting information emerged about coronavirus transmission, social service agencies began to call asking if I could join video conversations with their teams and staff to help demystify what was happening with the virus. After the first few sessions, I realized how terribly public health information was being communicated. People were confused about contact tracing, testing and clinical symptoms. They wanted guidance to understand when they should go to a hospital and how they would know if it was time. The public health guidance also discouraged people from going to hospitals, now seen as hotbeds of infection. So people didn't go, even if they desperately needed to.

Even though Grapevine Health had lost its funding, we could tell our mission as a company was more pressing than ever. Because I was out on the streets and talking to people in order to answer their questions and correct the misinformation I was hearing, I decided to resume filming Dr. Lisa on the Street again. I knew the conversations I was having could spread digitally and help more people learn about COVID-19 and take important steps to stay safe.

I also started a podcast to capture some of these stories I was hearing. The first person I interviewed was Lynette Roney,[70] a Black septuagenarian I met on a call with a senior at the Congress Heights Senior Wellness Center (CHSWC).[71] Pre-pandemic the organization incorporated a focus on digital literacy, and, therefore, when the lockdowns began, the shift to video programming was a natural evolution. The seniors were ready. I was invited to join a conversation and answer questions about the pandemic. It turned into a weekly engagement that enabled me to hear concerns and questions directly from seniors. They were engaged and hungry for information. Some consumed TV news voraciously and were well abreast of the pandemic and scientific information related to it. Others felt lost, uncertain, isolated or afraid. The pandemic occurred at the height of what had become known as the "loneliness" epidemic,[72] particularly for seniors. The pandemic and stay-home orders exacerbated loneliness, but for these seniors Zoom comradery softened the blow. Ms. Roney volunteered to tell her story on our podcast after I announced my interest in hearing directly from seniors. In our interview, she opened my eyes to the specific challenges we'd face nationally in gaining attention and trust from people in Black communities. I interviewed Ms. Roney three months after the initial pandemic declaration, and she told me she had not left her house in ninety days and had no plans to leave until, as she said, "The pandemic is over."

I asked, "What if you need to go to the hospital?" She said with conviction, "If somehow I get sick, I will not go to the hospital. I will die right here in my house." Stunned, I wanted to understand her reasons. She said, "Well, I heard they are putting old people in the corner when they get to the hospital. If they will do that to a white person, what do you think they will do to me? I'm old, I'm Black, and I'm a woman. There's no way I want to be left sitting in a corner to die."

There it was in her words: distrust of the healthcare system described as ageist, sexist and racist. As the pandemic unfolded, the world learned about the disproportionate impact of the pandemic on Black and brown people. I cannot count the number of times I was asked to explain these numbers. "Why are Black people dying at higher rates of COVID-19?" My initial instinct was to offer a snide response like, "The same reasons Black people are always dying disproportionately of everything else!" A wealth of data decades old elegantly highlight the connection between class, income—namely poverty—and social environment on the health outcomes and disease rates. When the pandemic arrived, despite knowing about and previously characterizing health and social disparities, we had no national solutions to mitigate the impact of poverty, structural racism[73] and social factors like consistent access to healthy foods, safe outdoor space and accessible, on-demand behavioral health services. Consequently, coronavirus visited the doorstep of millions of physically and mentally unwell Americans with little reserve to battle a new virus like SARS-CoV2. None of the statistics were surprising to me or to any of my public health and clinical colleagues at safety net health systems. These disparities had always been our reality, as we've had to make a way with little resources and do the best we could to provide care and support for underserved communities. The pandemic disparities would be no different but, in some cases, exponentially worse.

The health communication during this time was suboptimal and filled with jargon and speculation. As I listened to experts, I thought, "If you need to speculate, you *must* do a better job explaining *why* you are being vague." I was also appalled by some of the health department's responses. Typically, health departments don't regularly communicate and build relationships with the public. This means a crisis is *the* worst time to build relationships with the community and communicate critical health and public health messages. The most stark example I saw of the disconnect between public health officials and the public was in Rockland County, New York.[74] Given the lack of familiarity, communication and trust between the health department and the community, calls for participation in contact tracing were largely unheeded. Rather than modifying their communication approach to build trust, they instead criminalized failure to comply with contact-tracing requests. It was the best and worst display of how not to behave as public health officials.

Leaning on the Grapevine

From the beginning, the COVID-19 pandemic was fraught with distrust, conflicting messages and confusion.

Initially I was content to watch Dr. Fauci on Sunday news shows and edit him in my head as he occasionally selected a word I knew the general public would not understand. But I knew watching would not be enough, and that those of us in the medical community had to do more to connect with patients and bring clear and trustworthy information to the public, especially to those in underserved communities who, as I've shown, had many reasons to distrust healthcare professionals.

Although I had been studying this for years, the pandemic ushered in a surge of attention to the high levels of distrust of healthcare in the Black community. People were baffled by the initial low vaccine acceptance rate in the Black community. The Black community wasn't. Decision making in Black communities, not too dissimilar from most people, often relies on trusted messengers, whether it is a trusted social service organization that is a pillar in the community, a church or friends on a stoop bringing gossip from the bus stop.

In the Black community, for good reason, distrust of the healthcare system runs deep and wide. In her publication *Medical Apartheid*, Professor Harriet Washington chronicled the history of medical experimentation in the Black community.[75] These events and experiences are well known in the Black community, but during the pandemic we learned others were not so familiar with the legacy. I am still not sure why. People roll their eyes at the mention of things like slavery and past atrocities against Black and brown people, but eyerolling and dismissiveness cannot obscure an ugly history that has shaped the Black community's perspectives about healthcare and the decision making associated with it. Changing people's positions often requires a trusted messenger with a shared background and understanding.

If the pandemic taught me anything, it reinforced my belief that people want to receive health information in a language and manner that makes sense to them, and that they often want it delivered by someone who looks like and understands them. The absence of traditional healthcare and the ongoing neglect in the Black community led to countless stories passed on for generations about unequal healthcare treatment and access. Consequently, people resorted to trusted family messengers to address health concerns. There are people in my family able to recount tales of racism and discrimination encountered when attempting to access healthcare services. Given this, we should not be surprised the residue of these experiences has lingered. These experiences are not easily erased by one or even a few favorable encounters in healthcare. This means building trust requires consistent and intentional focus to prove commitment to trustworthiness in healthcare. Acknowledging a structural and deeply rooted problem in healthcare like racism feels overwhelming. I believe this is one reason I have encountered so many people in healthcare business and financing—people who control resources—who are skeptical that access to trusted health information can change lives, hearts and health outcomes— that a person hearing a message from someone who looks like and relates to them will shift their behavior. This has been a challenge for Grapevine Health business development, as the disbelievers are especially skeptical that health information delivered in the right manner via the right messenger can translate to a return on investment. But it is true and we saw this success repeatedly when the vaccines became available, as Grapevine Health came to play a direct and pivotal role in combatting vaccine hesitancy and getting more people in the Black community to agree to get vaccinated.

Street Outreach, Misinformation and Trusted Messengers

Several weeks into the pandemic, the misinformation and incessant phone calls and text messages forced me onto the street. The Grapevine Health team conducted street outreach and saw firsthand why Black people were dying of COVID-19 at disproportionate rates. The misinformation was rampant. We also learned people had variable access to masks and were baffled about how to isolate when sharing a space with family members. I spoke to a police officer who was afraid to go home after work because she lived with her mom so she would go shower at a friend's house. The media was blanketed with stories about healthcare workers and the creative ways they learned to protect their families, but after speaking to her, I realized no one was really talking about first responders. I called a friend at the fire department and heard the same. Except, what was more concerning was that according to him, many of the paramedics and firefighters didn't believe

COVID-19 was real. He also believed hospitals were falsifying diagnosis codes. This narrative was also on some news channels. Many people expressed that it was hard to know what to believe.

For a few months before vaccines became available, it felt as if we were not having much impact by conducting periodic outreach and listening to community concerns. But the availability of vaccines was a gamechanger for Grapevine Health.

We hit our stride when organizations began calling to ask if we could conduct virtual education for staff and frontline workers because the majority were skeptical about the vaccines and did not want to be vaccinated. I rallied seven or eight Black doctors to serve as trusted messengers and help with education. We eventually conducted dozens of in-person and virtual vaccine education sessions. We had no system established to track people and their vaccination status after our educational intervention. Instead, we relied on the CEOs and senior leaders of the organizations to provide estimates of the number of people who they believed were vaccinated as a result of Grapevine Health trusted messengers delivering vaccine education. The vaccine uptake rates ranged from thirty to seventy-five percent. This was proof that our model of direct engagement worked.

The most impressive impact we had was on a group of factory workers at a food distribution company. The supervisor called to inquire about Grapevine Health's education services and said that the workers were primarily thirty- to fifty-year-old Black men, none of whom wanted to be vaccinated. He was struggling with COVID-19 infections and the negative impact they were having on his workforce and supply chain. We deployed Dr. Dan Fagbuyi, a Black doctor, to deliver vaccine education on multiple shifts. A few days later the supervisor called and said he was amazed at the power of our trusted messenger approach. At that factory, they were offering gift cards as a vaccination incentive. Before Dr. Dan went to Atlanta, most of them went unclaimed. After his visit, the cards were all distributed and they called asking for more.

The media continued its obsession with the Tuskegee narrative and associated it with vaccine hesitancy.[76] In nearly every interview I gave for TV, radio and print, I was quizzed about it. This frustrated me for two reasons. First, it was not necessary to reach back decades to understand why Black people were distrustful of the healthcare system and research. As I shared with most of the interviewers, they could ask people about their treatment in healthcare today and understand the phenomenon of distrust and feeling mistreated and disrespected. Second, as more and more Black people were vaccinated and efforts among Black doctors escalated to educate the Black community and highlight our own vaccinations, vaccine hesitancy in the Black community was decreasing. But I suspect it was more sensational to talk about the Tuskegee legacy.

Entrepreneuring in a Pandemic

The pandemic, combined with George Floyd's murder, seemed to turn on philanthropic taps for Grapevine Health's business. Pre-pandemic these pipes seemed rusted and the flow of support was minimal. Not all investors understood the value of our mission, and even after we had secured our first contracts, we lost them when the pandemic started. Yet after the murder came what I call the sudden awakening—a global recognition that in many ways we are still living in a separate and unequal world. This was being borne out in the clinical and epidemiological data, which showed the pandemic communities hardest hit and least able to access timely care were Black and brown. But aside from national public health data, nowhere were these disparities more striking than in the worlds of philanthropy and venture capital. For months company after company and firm after firm released declarations about their commitment to justice and equality. The verbal support was unprecedented. Equity roundtables, diversity, equity and inclusion job descriptions and committees were springing up everywhere. Everyone seemed earnest about helping Black and brown people. In 2020, with little effort, Grapevine Health was granted nearly six hundred thousand dollars from philanthropic organizations that traditionally would not have given us the time of day because we are a social impact for-profit company. We used the funds to recruit other doctors to help address COVID-19 misinformation through street outreach, digital engagement, video content and webinars. We traveled to seven cities during the pandemic and could see the impact on the ground, as evidenced in increased vaccination rates. We also successfully competed for a highly coveted Small Business Innovation Research (SBIR) grant from the National Science Foundation, which required a considerable amount of work. We used these funds to begin implementing the next stage in our outreach plan: a texting strategy called HealthText to improve engagement among Medicaid enrollees and other populations who have been omitted from digital health innovation. Soon after receiving this support from SBIR, we landed our first contract, which was with a health system. We were asked to create tailored video content about COVID-19 testing and vaccines in English and Spanish. Other contracts followed with content requests. But these were all one-off engagements, and what I desired was a payer contract with an opportunity for repeatable business. The opportunity came a few months later from AmeriHealth Caritas DC.

AmeriHealth Caritas DC is a health plan that understood Grapevine Health could help them reach more of their members. We worked with them around diabetes and maternal health, interviewing patients to find out what steps they were taking—or in many cases, not taking—to see their doctors and seek preventive and follow-up care. We used the information we gathered in our interviews to create a series of videos encouraging people to see their doctors. These videos are not of people in white coats using medical jargon and 'scolding' patients into doing what they "should" do. Instead they feature regular people discussing their health and healthcare needs. For example in one video, an older Black woman named Ms. Brenda encourages people not to wait until they are her age to address their diabetes. As she tells the viewer, "We do more preventive maintenance on our cars than we do on our bodies. But now it's time for us diabetics and pre-diabetics to start getting our regular checkups." Messages from people like Ms. Brenda, a relatable community member struggling with a chronic health condition, are designed to deliver important healthcare information to Black and brown audiences by using technology to spread the word via video and text.

As we continued our qualitative data collection, community outreach and engagement, we also sought to elevate our video production quality and expand our text messaging capabilities. With a podcast, YouTube channel, and more doctors on the street, as well as a growing team, an advisory board, more partners and concrete plans to continue our expansion, the future was looking bright for Grapevine Health.

But in 2022 as the pandemic waned, money ran low. All donors who had so willingly supported Grapevine Health during the height of the pandemic informed us they were shifting back to business as usual. These organizations felt the pandemic was a once-in-a-lifetime occurrence and while they had wanted to pivot quickly to respond in 2020 and 2021, now that the pandemic was receding, they no longer saw the benefit or felt the urgency. Responses to funding requests mirrored those we'd received pre-pandemic. Our work fell outside their portfolio priorities. These responses were hard to process because we believed the lessons we'd learned and successes we'd enjoyed further validated Grapevine Health's mission to deliver trusted, relatable messages through trusted health messengers.

This need existed long before the pandemic and continues to outlive it. Trusted health information in the Black community is needed to address chronic health conditions that cost US taxpayers over four trillion dollars a year.[77] For people living outside the bubble of scarcity, poverty and inequitable access, life had returned to normal. For those living a life of poverty and inequity, the pandemic, as difficult and trying as it was, was merely a blip on the radar in a life full of stress, trauma, scarcity and neglect.

Although we had received significant funding from the NSF, it was not enough to fully launch our ambitious texting plan, HealthText. We had to keep searching for additional funding to continue our work designing and building this digital tool to uniquely engage Medicaid patients. In late 2022, we began to see the fruits of this labor. Our engagement was growing by several times. More people were watching and sharing our videos and seeking out our tools. We knew this would have a tangible impact on health outcomes and lead to an overall reduction in costs for health insurance companies and the US taxpayer. By 2023, we had multiple contracts with MCOs, an employer-based health insurer and were in talks with national insurers. After four years of bootstrapping, iterating, listening and networking, we could see the beginnings of our success.

But as much work as it has been, the work of transforming Grapevine Health into a relevant, scalable business that improves health outcomes for the poor and underserved its only beginning.

Part 3
Achieving Health Equity

No matter how far you have gone down a wrong
road, turn back.

Turkish proverb

Health Equity

The healthcare industry is truly enjoying a romance with
health equity. Health equity is the notion that everyone has
the resources and access they need to be the healthiest version
of themselves. The topic appears in documents, conferences,
webinars and leadership conversations everywhere. Given my
health disparities-related interests and leadership experience,
position descriptions for health equity directors have flooded
my inbox over the past two years, but little has changed.
My interviews with many new health equity vice presidents,
directors and associates reveal a largely frustrated group of
underutilized leaders with no budget, autonomy and authority to shift their organization's culture. Many of these people
know what to do but have no power to do it. Helping people

DOI: 10.4324/9781003243502-3   91 achieve their best health is complex. It requires commitments beyond inspirational speeches, conversations and health equity strategy plans with no mandate. Espousing a commitment to health equity while decrying the lack of actionable data as a barrier to its achievement is disingenuous. This book, along with many before and likely after it, is filled with examples describing how health inequity manifests inside and outside our healthcare institutions. The data we need lay right before us in people's stories about healthcare experiences, in service utilization patterns, in neighborhood and environmental influencers and in cultural norms that influence health and health behaviors. This information is available to us but we have to be willing to review and act upon it.

Acting upon it is challenging. Acting upon it can feel threatening. Do we want to change? A few years ago I met a young man born into a wealthy family. He accepted an internship in an impoverished community and, for the first time, was confronted with social disparities like food deserts, healthcare and education access and employment disparities that had been invisible to him. Frustrated by what he thought must be solvable problems, he asked me for career advice about how to use his wealth and influence to help address the disparities he was seeing. Instead of giving career advice, I challenged him to speak up about his experiences and what he had learned. I asked him to share his indignation with the embarrassing social disparities that made him restless. My suggestion made him uncomfortable. I asked, "Why is this so hard for you?" He was honest and said, "My life is good. I am not sure what would happen if I start speaking out about it."

This moral dilemma is also a driver of the status quo in healthcare. But the road we are traveling is so riddled with inequities it is becoming more and more challenging to remain on this path. We have to decide. Will we stay on an unjust path or find a new one?

Drivers of Health Inequity

Although I set out to focus on improving access to trusted health information and health literacy, the path has been winding with many detours that have forced me to consider how health literacy intersects with other health equity issues. It is discouraging to see how many drivers of avoidable utilization, like lack of access to education and prevention tools, are not being prioritized and funded but should be. The tragedy is that we know from experiences and research why people get sick—for example, distrust, low health literacy, limited access to preventive services and navigation support, and financial disparities requiring people to choose between employment and survival or preventive health behaviors. We also know a lot about which structural and environmental factors influence health. Foundations know these things. Health systems know these things. Even venture capitalists know these things. But healthcare is a business and pivoting away from this model to deliver care the way people need and shifting most of our efforts upstream to prevention and social drivers of health is daunting. This shift will require a bipartisan marketing and education campaign directed at communities, an energized public in urban and rural America and a sustained and unprecedented sectoral collaboration. It requires a movement akin to a multi-year, multi-state bipartisan political campaign. The demand must come from people with the most to lose if the system stays the same: the people who die younger and have higher rates of preventable health conditions. As Tony Benn points out, it is hard to participate in a revolution when you are poor, tired and hopeless—and when you feel the system is rigged. These are the reasons the current healthcare system persists, so we must work within the parameters we have and believe our incremental efforts will bring change.

Within this current system, if I were to change one thing, it would be the parameters established by the Centers for

Medicare and Medicaid Services (CMS) and insurers for what can be reimbursed and by whom. These are the most significant barriers to addressing healthcare challenges highlighted by what I have heard in my clinic, inbox, smartphone and on the street. According to them, some of the upstream factors that positively and negatively influence health and the decisions people make to engage in their health and with the healthcare system include:

Positive	Negative
Pain	Distrust
Loneliness	Past experiences (judgment, bias, racism, dismissiveness)
Fear of death	Fear of unknown
Curiosity ("Should I be worried?")	Fear of disease
Impatience (ED visits—"I want to be seen now")	Convenience
A desire for on-demand information	Lack of provider access (<72 hours) Unresponsive providers
Limited health literacy	Limited health literacy

People need easily accessible diagnostics, care, support and prevention tools. This is health equity. Because we lack a national strategy for addressing social drivers of health, including health literacy, and because there is no sustainable financing to address the drivers of engagement, health inequity will persist.

Another challenge for improving health outcomes and addressing health equity is how to address human problems like discrimination in diagnosing and treating health conditions. A wealth of research data documents the presence of separate and unequal access and outcomes in our healthcare system. For example, a recent study conducted by researchers at Brigham and Women's Hospital revealed differential access to life-saving heart failure interventions.[78] Black patients were consistently less likely to gain access to state-of-the-art heart failure care than white patients. When news of these studies reaches the community, the information reinforces existing perceptions and distrust. These problems persist because there is little accountability for identifying, publicizing and changing these practices.

These institutionalized norms are difficult to address because we perceive them as intangible, unmeasurable and unactionable. For example, how would a health system gauge whether or not someone is treated with dignity? There is no measure for dignity, but how people experience healthcare influences their decision to trust or engage in care. When I lived in Cambridge, Massachusetts, I needed a pap smear. I was referred to one of the elite hospital systems in Boston. The doctor who conducted my exam was a middle-aged white male who was curt and non-conversational. You might be inclined to give him a pass, attributing it to his personality. However, the doctor never smiled, didn't ask me questions, and got right to the pap smear as if I was inconveniencing him.

Because the procedure involves using a lubricant, which is usually messy and runny, after conducting a pap smear, it is customary and courteous to provide something to clean oneself after the procedure. The doctor finished the procedure, stood up, informed me the exam was complete, left the room without inviting me to ask questions or make a follow-up appointment and left me to figure out how to remove the lubricant from my body. Solutions for addressing a situation like this include speaking to someone immediately about the experience, writing a complaint, evaluating the experience in a survey or never returning. I complained before I left, but the more important question is, what could be done to change this doctor's heart and perception of me? He was not happy to be my doctor. Why? What was it about me? Would he have treated me differently if I had been a white woman? We can never know the answers to these questions in a way that would enable us to direct interventions effectively.

And for this reason, we can only solve these problems by hiring and training future generations to practice in a way that recognizes and validates the dignity of all patients. Ultimately, from the top to the bottom of healthcare institutions, we need to hire for empathy, compassion and humanity and figure out how to reward these behaviors. We will unlikely repair the trust gaps between Black and brown communities and health systems until we figure this out.

Ultimately, this is why organizations like Grapevine Health are critical and pivotal. Knowing that Black people most often prefer to receive their health information from Black doctors might be hard to accept, particularly for predominantly white, esteemed and academic elite institutions run by people with no social or cultural similarity to people requiring their services. Yet data show this is true. During the pandemic, I was introduced to leaders at two Fortune 500 institutions seeking solutions for improving vaccination rates among their Black employees. The suggestion that Black doctors could better deliver trusted health messages to their Black employees who were vaccine-hesitant was dismissed as simplistic and redundant. In one case, the Chief Medical Officer responded by saying their institution had over ten thousand doctors to choose from who were capable of delivering vaccine education to employees. This dismissiveness of tailored messages from trusted, relatable messengers is among the most significant business threats for Grapevine Health and our ability to scale the approach to reach underserved Black and brown communities around the US. We at Grapevine Health know the community we are working with and the best way to reach Black and brown employees and underserved patients in exactly the ways insurers and employers are seeking, yet for this outreach to be successful it will require a true investment in the solutions we offer.

There is also little urgency to reach the health equity milestones that show we are making sustainable progress. At the Kennedy School, when learning about startup culture, a common phrase cited in innovation was that you must "go fast and break things." However, in healthcare circles, the refrain suggests this cannot apply because "if you go fast and break things in healthcare, people die." The phrase caught on, so the industry seems complacent with the notion that changing healthcare and improving outcomes moves at a glacial pace, despite the unabated morbidity and mortality from preventable health conditions.

We saw during the pandemic and after the murder of George Floyd that funding existed for our mission. We know insurance companies, employers and government agencies are looking for ways to encourage preventive healthcare and services to reduce expensive and time-consuming interventions later on. Yet if those who control the purse strings continue to primarily fund tech-based "solutions" at the expense of direct, community-based outreach, there will be no progress toward achieving health equity. Poor engagement in care and preventive health behaviors is expensive for the healthcare system. This costly problem is perpetuated by the current culture of healthcare financing, which is resistant to change and to the iteration of strategies that can capture attention, build trust and improve engagement among those who need the most support.

Lessons in Innovation

Through rich engagement with patients and communities, the Grapevine Health journey, which started with a specific focus on health literacy, has blossomed to address the intersection of multiple areas of healthcare innovations, including trust, social determinants of health, digital health innovation and health communication. The lessons learned about each suggest that achieving health equity will be possible only by incorporating focused action in these areas.

Trust

Our community engagements validate that trust is foundational to engagement in care, yet it needs to be addressed in conversations about healthcare transformation. But how do we build a trusted healthcare system, particularly for underserved patients? A few actions can help move us forward.

Building trust starts outside four walls. The commonly espoused approach of "meeting people where they are" has little sustainable impact if community members never see representatives from local health institutions in their environment. Getting proximal and being seen in the community sends a message of sincerity and builds bridges. A few years ago, an advisory board at the National Institutes of Health (NIH) solicited suggestions about increasing the enrollment of diverse populations in clinical trials. I advised sending researchers into the community to educate, listen and use the information to establish a non-academic trial site in the neighborhood. The historical distrust and community suspicion associated with research remains prevalent, and these perceptions influence engagement in routine healthcare. Showing up in the community is a significant first step.

Also, we need to talk less and listen more. When patients enter care, the initial clinical interview—the history—can be overwhelming and feel like an interrogation. If tailored appropriately, the history can be transformed into an empathic exchange that builds trust. What if we re-imagine the clinical history and instead of starting with questions about the nature and duration of the medical complaint, the first question is about the patients' deepest fears and skepticism about seeking care or past experiences that influence their perceptions about care? What if we started with probes like, "I understand it may have been tough for you to come here. Thank you for making an effort. First, tell me your biggest concern about being here." Or, "What matters most to you about your health?" These prompts can help establish trust and assist in allaying fear, which is among the most significant barriers to engagement in care.

Another influencer of trust is the interaction with healthcare staff. Frontline administrative staff, like greeters and intake staff, can set the tone for a patient's healthcare experience. Yet Medicaid patients often report experiencing condescension and judgment from staff. Thus, the healthcare workforce must be trained to value and embody trust. This includes addressing bias against certain patients. When patients enter our institutions with expectations formed long before arrival, it will take little to reinforce their perceptions. Each negative interaction, no matter how subtle or unintentional, validates their skepticism and further erodes trust bit by bit. Long term, adequately addressing trust as a driver of health outcomes requires us to measure, reward and hold our systems accountable. As the surge in health innovation and systems transformation efforts continues, it's vitally important we recognize this critical driver.

Social Determinants of Health

Social determinants of health (SDOH) are now widely accepted as influential in health outcomes.[79] While they must be considered in devising healthcare interventions, we have learned that incorporating them to improve health outcomes is only possible with a long-term commitment to addressing a few social and cultural challenges.

First, transportation benefits are vital for some people but cannot replace trust. One of the most tangible and measurable

SDOH-related interventions is improving access to transportation. In many primary care clinics serving people experiencing poverty, the no-show rates are persistently high, and some of these missed appointments are reportedly due to a lack of transportation. Many health systems and insurance carriers now provide non-emergency medical transportation to healthcare visits to address this challenge.[80,81] However, participants in our discussion groups who discussed transportation benefits suggested the reasons for not keeping appointments had little to do with transportation and that if they felt the visit was essential, they could identify options for attending healthcare visits. Some shared negative experiences with the healthcare system and reported the single biggest determinant of returning for follow-up was the relationship with the provider and the health system environment. We interviewed a Medicaid beneficiary who told us she appreciated the ride-share benefit but had a car and her reason for repeat ED visits was related to her provider's inability to diagnose and treat her health condition.

Second, low food literacy must be addressed. While people often understand the link between food and good health, knowing how to select and prepare food can be challenging. This must be addressed to achieve long-term benefits from food interventions. Consistent and sustainable food education is essential and deserves investment. This includes identification of foods, reading and understanding food labels and skills development to prepare meals. Modifying food-related policies to facilitate access is a critical step,[82] but the impact of these changes will only be realized if we also shift the food culture and perspectives about healthy food relative to the food choices persistently available in poor communities. Some community members with multiple chronic conditions expressed their preferences for fast food and carry-out options over fresh fruits and vegetables. These preferences were linked to flavor rather than cost. Thus, although improving access to conveniently located healthy food is imperative for good health, community-wide adoption of healthy food choices will require a gradual shift in the community's palate and a change in how low-income communities think about and value food.

Finally, poverty and lack of economic opportunity are driving health inequities. Many people we have encountered are disengaged from their health and the healthcare system because their economic survival is in constant competition with what they perceive as non-immediate threats like health. Both Black and Hispanic community members shared these views. In some cases, examples highlight how lack of job and financial security forced them to delay healthcare needs. Gig workers and day laborers described prolonged delays in seeking medical care for fear that missed work days meant lost opportunities for future employment because another worker would immediately replace them. For the poor, desperate financial need clouds the ability to prioritize health, particularly when most preventable health conditions are often intangible and thus perceived as non-threatening. The need to address economic security to achieve better health outcomes is increasingly recognized, leading to a movement exploring medical financial partnerships.[83] This approach is a new paradigm for the US but could revolutionize the delivery of social, economic and medical integration of service delivery.

Integrating SDOH interventions into healthcare delivery will likely nudge some individual health outcomes. However, deep investments in SDOH solutions suggest a belief among many that addressing them is *the* answer to our long-sought but elusive health outcomes for low-income populations. Our community engagement instead indicates a need to continue evaluating our approaches to and expectations from SDOH interventions. This is because achieving population-based shifts in health outcomes for low-income communities requires moving far beyond text message reminders, Uber rides to clinic visits and vouchers for farmers markets and food pantries. These shifts demand bold and transformative steps to address poverty by providing education, economic opportunity and a pathway to lifelong financial stability.

Digital Innovation

According to Rock Health, year after year, the digital health sector enjoys lucrative investments with billions invested each year.[84] However, despite nearly eight hundred billion dollars spent annually in Medicaid programs, investment to spur digital health innovation for Medicaid patients is sluggish compared to those for self-paying and privately insured health consumers.

In our discussions with founders, investors and funders, some misperceptions and myths about the Medicaid population and the financial opportunity for return on investment (ROI) from Medicaid innovation are inaccurate. Some of these myths include:

1. The risk isn't worth the reward. Medicaid programs are overly bureaucratic with little opportunity to realize an ROI.
2. Grants from foundations and non-profit organizations best support socially driven companies.
3. Underserved communities lack sufficient access to the Internet and technology.

Bureaucracy can stifle Medicaid programs because, unlike Medicare, which is also bureaucratic, Medicaid is administered by states and, thus, can dissuade investors from pursuing individualized, time-consuming, state-by-state approaches to innovation. Even so, these companies forgo billions of dollars in ROI opportunities every year because they perceive the risk and required effort as too great.

The notion that innovation for Medicaid patients should be primarily funded by grants allocated to non-profit organizations is myopic and stifles the ability to create sustainable, root cause-driven impact. Grant funding is also inappropriate for supporting long-term health systems transformation because it is time-limited and unsustainable. Furthermore, the burden of securing and managing grants detracts from program implementation because employees must expend time and efforts toward applying for funding instead of implementing the work of the organization. Many funders are reluctant to give money to groups they perceive as having too much overhead, without recognizing that money must be spent to attract and pay the salaries of capable employees and establish the infrastructure needed for their success. Companies with socially driven missions require capital to build and implement sustainable revenue models that endure beyond a grant cycle. When a company like Grapevine Health no longer must divert its time and attention to identifying one-off funding opportunities, it can dedicate its focus to developing a relevant, profitable and scalable product that helps people while reducing costs.

The pervasive perception that the poor lack access to technology is inexplicable. A wealth of research data from reputable organizations like Pew Research Center highlight why mobile phone, including smartphone, access is no longer a barrier to innovation for the underserved.[85] Nearly ninety percent of Americans can access public Wi-Fi and a mobile phone. Additionally, smartphone ownership is at an all-time high, even among people experiencing poverty. Furthermore, in underserved communities worldwide, mobile devices are imperative for millions who rely on them to communicate via text, complete job applications, conduct financial transactions, summon ride-share services, browse social media and source information via the Internet. This is true even for many people experiencing homelessness. Over the years, we have received text messages from people who are reachable only by cell phone and have successfully connected them to relevant health information and resources.

A common explanation for low investment in innovation for the underserved is a perception that the health technologies being developed will eventually "trickle down" to underserved populations. The digital health revolution started over ten years ago and has yet to trickle down and significantly improve outcomes for the poor. Furthermore, these technologies are being developed without the context and language needed to benefit the underserved. Thus, if they trickle down, it is unclear how useful the technologies will be if not designed for a specific context. Guarding against omission from technology advancements and adverse outcomes from tech access disparities requires focus, intention and inclusion—the inclusion of patients and experts to help inform discovery, testing and implementation methods. We must adopt a more creative mindset to address these challenges and ensure digital health investments increase reach into underserved communities.

We also need to recognize that in the same way that digital resources do not "trickle down" to underserved populations, other improvements to healthcare will not "trickle down" either. I cannot count how many conversations I have had with well-meaning people who suggest Grapevine Health would be better off and better positioned to secure funding opportunities if we stopped focusing on Black and brown communities. They tell me I will have more success by focusing on white majority and financially-able populations, first demonstrating value in these markets. Their reasoning is that this approach will then "trickle down" to those who are living in poverty and on the margins, many of whom are insured by Medicaid. But we have seen time and time again that this approach does not work. Therefore, I have been intentional about focusing our efforts on people that are continually left behind, particularly by digital health innovation, choosing not to wait for solutions that will not work in underserved communities and unlikely to ever reach them at all.

I believe there is opportunity in our community-centered approach. Because health tech is a relatively new space, innovators and investors still have the chance to engage underserved communities in designing and deploying digital health tools that reach these populations directly. While the access could be better and may not achieve every healthcare goal, it is certainly good enough to ensure the most vulnerable aren't continually left behind.

Health Communication

Throughout the pandemic, nearly all of Grapevine Health's work and community engagement has involved listening to the community—on the street, virtually during Ask the Doctor[86] sessions, through hearsay and even reading text messages. A mother once texted me while sitting in a clinic waiting for her son's vaccination to obtain my reassurance that she was making the right decision to have him vaccinated. Examples like this can provide insights about how and why efforts to communicate complex health information in underserved communities are not resonating. We aim to learn from these missed opportunities and demonstrate the impact of community-driven health communication. We also see from these interactions what solutions are most needed, like HealthText, videos, our YouTube channel and other creative ways of soliciting community engagement.

Communities are now more attuned to health, science and medicine information than ever before. Last year we asked patients about sources of trusted health information and learned how badly conflicting health information eroded trust in health systems. Health communication was also perceived as dishonest because evolving information was treated as certain. Several people have related their disinterest in the scientific presentation of data and prefer to engage with relatable visuals and videos. Above all, it is well-established by now that trusted messengers are most valued for delivering actionable health information and can make a tangible difference in how people seek care and in the bottom line for both insurers and employers.

We also learned people are often perplexed by science and its processes and do their best to assimilate complex health and scientific information. Our Ask the Doctor sessions provide insight into how our health communication could be more effectively reaching and educating many communities about the basics of science, research and medicine. Therefore, we must find ways to deliver health information that is nuanced and tailored by context to help people understand the "how" and "why" of science and medicine. The use of metaphors and analogies is very effective.

Because health and science communicators take the listener's knowledge for granted too often, people often express a need to conduct their "own research." This process requires sifting through online medical and scientific jargon, leaving them to draw conclusions that may need to be corrected. A man who told me he does his own research described his process as Google first, followed by reading abstracts from Medline searches and consulting an online medical dictionary for words he does not understand. Afterward, he shares his conclusions among people he believes are more intelligent than he is. His health decisions are ultimately based upon whatever seems most logical for him. His process conjured courtroom images with lawyers battling for the jury's attention. It validates the need to deliver credible, more relatable, simplified, and jargon-free health information. More than ever, there is a glaring need to address the community's health information and social support needs, especially for the vulnerable.

We are losing misinformation and disinformation wars and leaving the community vulnerable to misinformation. This is partially because credible science messengers are less abundant and relentless than purveyors of misinformation in conveying health information through non-traditional or new media information channels. It is also because we must consistently dialogue with communities to understand their fears, concerns and misperceptions about science.

Addressing Health Equity: The Way Forward

On May 27, 2022, I encountered a man on the street who was homeless and recently discharged from the hospital. When I approached I could see him wearing his hospital wrist band, which made me curious, so I stopped to talk with him. My interaction with him can serve as a case study to examine health system challenges and design strategies to move us toward health equity. After that encounter, I posted my third most viral tweet with a photo of his hands showing the hospital wristband. It read:

> Who are these hard to reach people? Colleagues often ask me for tips on how to engage the hard to reach. Just now walking into Sweetgreen, a man asked if I had change. I told him I never carry money nowadays since so much is done w/ the phone. I asked if he wanted something to eat. He nodded, and I told him I would see if I could order it on my phone. Intrigued he said, Really? How do you do that? This led to a conversation as we waited 15 minutes for his food. Here is what I learned about him in less than 15 min:
> Born and lived in DC til he was six; doesn't have a phone, sleeps in different parks; limited reading

ability; doesn't have a watch; likes chicken and vegetables; never heard of quinoa; lost his ID; went to human services center but was refused services because he didn't have an ID. I stayed with this conversation about the service center for a few minutes to understand what happened. In a nutshell, there were too many steps to get help, which required him to go to different places but he didn't have transportation money. Recently hospitalized but could only tell me they gave him an injection and he has some kind of cancer. Doesn't have a doctor. Upon discharge, he doesn't recall being assigned assistance post hospitalization. Doesn't have Medicaid because he doesn't have an ID. Spent 26 years in prison, released several months ago but no one has helped him navigate his way through the healthcare system. He said he still wears the hospital wristband because he doesn't have an ID. Look at that list and ask yourself if he was hard to reach. After all, he was just sitting there, right out in the open. He made eye contact and asked me a question. Easiest connection ever. #humanity

This interaction reminds me of the Sir Osler quote: "Listen to the patient, he is telling you the diagnosis."

This encounter points us to problems and solutions for addressing health inequity and closing access gaps. In the US, organizations, companies and health systems spend billions on consulting, working group convenings and stakeholder analyses to identify, characterize and re-brand problems we are well acquainted with. The encounter also represents how we must address bureaucratic barriers to access health and social support for underserved communities and people insured by Medicaid. It demonstrates our perpetuation of overly complex and non-human-centered processes, the ways we exacerbate loneliness and isolation, our failures to address food and shelter insecurity and the many missed opportunities to close the "digital divide." I meet people like him at least once a week. They have taught me that the solutions are right in front of us if we have the will to depart from business as usual, make tough decisions, demand accountability for service that reaches the people who need it and examine our funding and resource decisions. The way forward to addressing health inequity will require specific and intentional action. These include:

1. Build trust with the community. Get out of the office. I am often asked about the best way to build trust in the Black community. These questions generally come from people who are culturally dissimilar and feel intimidated about engaging in outreach to Black and underserved communities. Building trust means showing up in a non-transactional way—you are not there because you want to extract data or one-off participation in a research study—and treating people with respect. This is difficult for many people because policy mandates often demand engagement, making the engagement coerced rather than authentic and altruistically motivated. Intentions are easily identifiable. If you are a leader who is not naturally inclined to outreach or engagement in underserved communities, identify people who support this work and deputize them with the authority to build trust with the community. In healthcare, the methods by which we are trained to interact with patients and the community are inherently paternalistic, authoritarian and judgmental. The irony is that people seeking care and support desire and need just the opposite.
2. Train doctors and other allied health professionals to lead with humanism. The academic demands of those training for healthcare professions can be overwhelming. The

curricula and educational requirements have become politicized, overemphasizing academic achievement like board scores. This creates a healthcare workforce that is disconnected from, inept at and in some cases disinterested in community engagement. As a colleague Rushika Fernandopulle told me, "We need to figure out how to decrease the social distance between doctors and patients." He is right, but the gap and distrust will persist until we prioritize this in graduate medical education.

3. Embed trauma and poverty concepts in curricula. Because these factors are often integrally linked with health outcomes in underserved populations, healthcare providers must become equipped to recognize and refer people for support. Until there is a national, cohesive strategy to address poverty, healthcare providers and health systems must play a role in mitigating the health-related impacts of these socially driven health influencers.

4. Invest in prevention and upstream health interventions. The gentleman I spoke with on the street had a cancer diagnosis and would likely end up back in the hospital if he could not access social support after his hospitalization. This avoidable hospitalization is one of the biggest pain points for insurance companies. Providing the necessary social services would be beneficial for the gentleman because he would get the support he needs, and it would be cost-effective for the insurer because providing a "helper" to assist him would cost less than repeat hospital stays. Even without a chronic disease diagnosis, many people without housing rely on the emergency room for support that could be provided by a well-organized and accessible social safety net. Over the past few years, we have witnessed a surge in social support-based companies that offer access to upstream services like transportation, food, housing and employment assistance. However, we have seen little shift in disparities trends. This is

likely due to a lack of collaboration and coordination of upstream services. Most social support businesses operate in parallel to or outside the local and state government systems that provide this support. What is missing is a well-publicized, recognized and harmonized system that is easily accessible. Any service that requires too many steps, requirements or rules to follow will go underutilized. We must make upstream services and processes much simpler and easier to access and use.

5. Understand payment barriers and advocate for change. The Centers for Medicare and Medicaid Services governs payment for hospitals and healthcare providers. Specifically, we need to advocate for CMS reimbursement for Medicaid services, particularly sub-specialty care, to match reimbursement for Medicare services and incentivize healthcare providers to provide care for those insured by Medicaid. In addition, the metrics CMS uses to determine payment are generally not linked directly to the services needed to close care gaps. For example, the gentleman on the street needed a care navigator, food and a place to stay. Otherwise, he would end up back in the hospital. In a health-equity-focused world, his social needs would be reimbursed for providing the support he needs to stay healthy. As healthcare-related businesses emerge, companies are first guided by how to get paid rather than by who needs help and how. This leads companies to expend time and resources following flawed regulations and policies rather than advocating for human needs and benefits, even though a patient-centered approach would save those companies significantly more money in the long-term. We must better understand the drivers of reimbursement policy decisions that leave people behind. There is a clear roadmap to pay for the gentleman's hospitalizations but how to get paid for the care he needs to stay out of the hospital is unclear. Often

"regulation" is cited as the most significant barrier to these policy shifts, but knowing which regulations *specifically* need to change is murky to the average healthcare stakeholder. Clarifying these regulations will make it easier to establish and advocate for the specific payment policies that move us closer to health equity. Once we identify and outline such regulations and processes, we will be in a better position to collectively understand which actions are needed to shift to regulations that help people get better care and support. Advocating to better understand how and why CMS is governed the way it is would advance health equity because the transparency and insight would focus, motivate and shift attention to specific reimbursement hurdles for upstream and preventive services. Ultimately, the unspoken flaw in all of this is that a congressional regulation might be the greatest barrier to people accessing the resources they need to be healthy and productive.

6. Develop seamless communication channels and messaging to address community health information and engagement needs. We can start by consistently listening to the community to deeply understand the experiences that inform their beliefs and acceptance or rejection of credible health information. The more we know about how and why we fail to deliver impactful health and science information, the better we can respond.

7. Eliminate science elitism—the idea that the most credible science is basic science accomplished using a microscope or at the research bench via pipetting and cell culture. There is more to science than microscopes, pipettes and cell culture. Science is nearly everywhere and in everything—health, medicine, public health research and even technology. To more effectively reach the community with credible, data-driven health and science information, we must disrupt the culture of

science elitism and the judgment and bias against communicating through more relatable and engaging strategies. Academics and policymakers often speak in jargon void of concrete, actionable information and generally talk to each other rather than the community. In addition, although many people, particularly in underserved communities, rely on social and digital media engagement for health information, these information sources are generally viewed as less credible and authoritative, as if educating and engaging through these channels is beneath us. We must change this and bridge communication gaps between scientists, policymakers and the community. This includes showing up in the community with authenticity, humility, openness and humanity. We can do this directly or through partnerships. Either way, unless we heed these lessons, the trust deficit will remain when the next pandemic happens upon us, and we will see we have made no progress at all.

Epilogue

In September 2022, Oliver Wyman invited me to deliver a keynote address at their annual Health Innovation Summit. To introduce me, they played a Dr. Lisa on the Street video. I had created the video specifically for them to address the conference theme, which focused on community knowledge about new technologies and science. I asked people on the street in a beach town if they understood terms like machine learning, genomics, precision medicine and artificial intelligence. I also asked them if they trusted these new technologies. No one I spoke to understood the practical implications of these innovations for the future of healthcare. The video message was an endorsement of our work at Grapevine Health. People from all walks of life crave access to relatable, trustworthy health information. For my presentation, I was given a license to speak the truth about the journey I'd been on with Grapevine Health. Aided by examples and recordings from people I've met along the way, I emphasized the need to better engage humans, particularly those from underserved communities, in healthcare innovation. I had nothing to lose, so I unabashedly shared my frustration about the obsession with data collection and analytics over meeting people's basic needs. I also talked about the disconnect I see between what health system leaders say they want, who they are contracting with and listening to and what is being funded. I highlighted the connection between distrust and poor health outcomes and the missed opportunity to address health literacy by supporting companies like Grapevine Health. Over the following weeks, several organizations reached out to learn more about Grapevine Health.

A few months later, the award-winning health policy podcast, Tradeoffs, interviewed me to talk about my journey building Grapevine Health. Their comprehensive approach to healthcare storytelling led them into the home of a community member impacted by our work and the office of a payor contracting for our services. Attracting the attention of a high-profile and well-respected media outlet and personality like Dan Gorenstein is a signal we are on the right track.[87]

I hope this is a new era of scale and partnerships for Grapevine Health and other companies like ours that aim to focus upstream before people struggle with life-threatening preventable illnesses that cost taxpayers trillions of dollars. One thing I know to be true is we are on a path that is validated by the people we serve. I only hope our healthcare system can soon pivot away from the things we know don't work, embrace new ideas and new thinking and follow the community's lead. After all, no one knows better what it takes to create healthy communities than they do.

Albert Einstein said, "Problems cannot be solved with the same mindset that created them." This is our challenge in creating a more health-equitable system. It's time for courage and bravery. We must be brave enough to loosen the reins, listen, let go a bit and let the community lead us. After all, they are humanity. They are the true trusted messengers. Without this mindset, there will never be health equity.

Notes

1. https://100blackmen.org/
2. https://www.linkedin.com/in/william-a-cooper-md-mba/
3. https://grapevinehealth.com
4. https://archpublichealth.biomedcentral.com/articles/10.1186/s13690-021-00648-7
5. https://www.ncbi.nlm.nih.gov/pmc/articles/PMC3785182/
6. https://nam.edu/
7. https://nap.nationalacademies.org/download/10883
8. https://www.ncbi.nlm.nih.gov/books/NBK216029/
9. https://theconversation.com/medical-jargon-is-often-misunderstood-by-the-general-public-new-study-195606
10. https://pubmed.ncbi.nlm.nih.gov/18452047/
11. https://www.sciencedaily.com/releases/2018/11/181107130314.htm
12. https://proliteracy.org/Blogs/Article/308/4-Cold-Hard-Facts-About-Health-Literacy
13. https://www.ncbi.nlm.nih.gov/pmc/articles/PMC4629700/
14. https://www.reuters.com/article/us-health-medical-marketing/u-s-health-care-industry-spends-30-billion-a-year-on-marketing-idUSKCN1P22GG
15. https://www.forbes.com/sites/lisafitzpatrick/2019/03/18/got-trust-we-are-ignoring-a-vital-predictor-of-engagement-in-care/?sh=7aacabc91eef
16. https://www.ncbi.nlm.nih.gov/pmc/articles/PMC4689381/
17. https://www.sciencedirect.com/science/article/abs/pii/S2213177919308716?via%3Dihub#!

18. https://nam.edu/perspectives-2015-health-literacy-a-necessary-element-for-achieving-health-equity/
19. https://www.businessinsider.com/why-insurers-are-afraid-of-social-media-companies-2010-11
20. https://www.mckinsey.com/industries/healthcare-systems-and-services/our-insights/digital-is-reshaping-us-health-insurance-winners-are-moving-fast
21. https://www.mckinsey.com/industries/healthcare-systems-and-services/our-insights/digital-is-reshaping-us-health-insurance-winners-are-moving-fast
22. https://health.gov/healthypeople/priority-areas/social-determinants-health/literature-summaries/food-insecurity
23. https://health.gov/healthypeople/priority-areas/social-determinants-health
24. https://jamanetwork.com/journals/jamainternalmedicine/article-abstract/2730764
25. https://www.geisinger.org/freshfoodfarmacy
26. https://www.feedingamerica.org/partners/food-and-fund-partners/visionary-partners/elevance-health-foundation
27. https://jamanetwork.com/journals/jamainternalmedicine/article-abstract/2553293
28. https://www.ncbi.nlm.nih.gov/pmc/articles/PMC4025682/
29. https://doi.org/10.1093/ajcn/26.11.1180
30. https://www.cdc.gov/heartdisease/facts.htm
31. https://www.springer.com/gp/about-springer/media/research-news/all-english-research-news/wait--just-a-second--is-your-doctor-listening-/15963052
32. https://www.youtube.com/watch?v=WJlY9C7YWzI
33. https://www.youtube.com/watch?v=QO8fyzBC2p8
34. https://www.youtube.com/watch?v=ThIKurq1oZg&t=
35. https://www.huffpost.com/entry/away-with-aids_b_2625271
36. https://jamanetwork.com/journals/jamanetworkopen/fullarticle/2772682
37. https://journals.sagepub.com/doi/full/10.1177/1077558719860708
38. https://www.kff.org/policy-watch/advancing-health-equity-requires-more-better-data/
39. https://dchealth.dc.gov/sites/default/files/dc/sites/doh/publication/attachments/DC%20Health%20Systems%20Plan%202017_0.pdf

40. https://www.forbes.com/sites/lisafitzpatrick/2018/11/16/the
    -emergency-department-is-healthcares-one-night-stand-are-we
    -ready-to-address-it/?sh=5b607c1c32eb
41. https://psycnet.apa.org/doiLanding?doi=10.1037%2Fh0054346
42. https://www.cms.gov/CCIIO/Programs-and-Initiatives/Health
    -Insurance-Market-Reforms/Medical-Loss-Ratio
43. https://medium.com/@askdrfitz/sorry-your-app-wont-work
    -three-reasons-the-digital-health-community-is-getting-it-wrong
    -ef611173d3a7
44. https://www.commonwealthfund.org/
45. https://www.fcc.gov/reports-research/working-papers/digital
    -divide-us-mobile-technology-and-speeds
46. https://www.himss.org/resources/digital-divide-healthcare-its
    -not-just-access
47. https://www.youtube.com/watch?v=KQ02iWTPmrM&t=
48. https://www.pewtrusts.org/en/research-and-analysis/blogs/
    stateline/2015/2/24/states-strive-to-keep-medicaid-patients-out
    -of-the-emergency-department
49. https://harriettubmanbyway.org/harriet-tubman/
50. https://www.medicaid.gov/medicaid/program-information/med-
    icaid-and-chip-enrollment-data/report-highlights/index.html
51. https://files.kff.org/attachment/fact-sheet-medicaid-state-DC
52. https://www.abfe.org/wp-content/uploads/2016/11/The
    -Health-of-the-African-American-Community-in-the-District-of
    -Columbia.pdf
53. https://www.georgetown.edu/news/report-shows-huge-d-c
    -health-disparities-makes-recommendations/
54. https://ourhealthydc.org/dc-chna/
55. https://www.washingtonpost.com/opinions/2022/10/26/dc-at
    -large-races-significant-undervoting-ward-7-ward-8/
56. https://www.ncbi.nlm.nih.gov/pmc/articles/PMC7147972/
57. https://pubmed.ncbi.nlm.nih.gov/1467758/
58. https://pubmed.ncbi.nlm.nih.gov/32122559/#:~:text=Adverse
    %20childhood%20experiences%20%28ACEs%29%20are
    %20stressful%20or%20traumatic,clear%20opportunity%20for
    %20early%20detection%2C%20intervention%2C%20and
    %20treatment.
59. https://patientengagementhit.com/features/how-rideshare-com-
    panies-can-address-social-determinants-of-health

60. https://www.ers.usda.gov/webdocs/publications/45014/30940
    _err140.pdf
61. https://www.youtube.com/watch?v=37wkX2gklzo
62. https://www.kff.org/other/state-indicator/health-insurance-cov-
    erage-of-the-total-population-cps/?currentTimeframe=0&sort-
    Model=%7B%22colId%22:%22Location%22,%22sort%22:%22asc
    %22%7D
63. https://www.fqhc.org/what-is-an-fqhc
64. https://www.ncbi.nlm.nih.gov/pmc/articles/PMC4833089/
65. https://www.aspeninstitute.org/programs/aspen-global-leader-
    ship-network/
66. https://www.nejm.org/doi/full/10.1056/NEJMoa2001191
67. https://www.cdc.gov/malaria/about/history/history_cdc.html
68. https://www.cdc.gov/eis/
69. https://www.forbes.com/sites/lisafitzpatrick/2020/04/02/covid
    -19-and-the-underserved-we-are-not-all-in-this-together/?sh
    =14da6e825a71
70. https://grapevinehealth.com/ms-roney/
71. https://www.fsfsc.org/congress-heights-senior-wellness-ce
72. https://www.cdc.gov/aging/publications/features/lonely-older
    -adults.html
73. https://www.ama-assn.org/delivering-care/health-equity/what
    -structural-racism
74. https://thehill.com/policy/healthcare/505437-new-york-county
    -issues-subpoenas-to-people-refusing-to-talk-to-contact/
75. https://www.mahoganybooks.com/9780767915472
76. https://www.sciencedirect.com/topics/medicine-and-dentistry/
    tuskegee-syphilis-experiment
77. https://www.cdc.gov/chronicdisease/about/costs/index.htm
78. https://www.ncbi.nlm.nih.gov/pmc/articles/PMC7183732/
79. https://www.cdc.gov/about/sdoh/index.html#:~:text=Social
    %20determinants%20of%20health%20(SDOH,the%20
    conditions%20of%20daily%20life.
80. https://www.cms.gov/medicare-medicaid-coordination/fraud
    -prevention/medicaid-integrity-program/education/non-emer-
    gency-medical-transport
81. https://www.cms.gov/medicare-medicaid-coordination/fraud
    -prevention/medicaid-integrity-education/downloads/nemt
    -booklet.pdf

82. https://www.publichealthlawcenter.org/topics/food-justice
83. https://prosperitynow.org/events/medical-financial-partnerships -exploring-successful-models
84. https://rockhealth.org/insights/
85. https://www.pewresearch.org/internet/fact-sheet/mobile/
86. https://grapevinehealth.com/askthedoctor/
87. https://tradeoffs.org/2023/02/02/health-literacy-disparities-lisa -fitzpatrick

Acknowledgments

Thank you to those who supported and inspired the work of Grapevine Health. This includes:

My editor Kristine Mednansky, thank you for your support and for recognizing the importance of Grapevine Health.

My family.

My patients and community members who taught me humility and how to listen.

Grapevine Health's first donor, David Gavrich.

Grapevine Health's Go Fund Me donors who believed in our mission before most:

Renee Ridzon, Sue Griffey, Rick Gilfillan, Jenny Delwood, Anika Hobbs, Ewunike Akpan, Ian Galloway, Yasmin Khan, Alison Rhein, Jay Duhig, Renee Tedesco (RIP), Debbie Weil, Shirlene Warnock, Robyn Jones, Paula Belikove, Dawn Hutchinson, Sarah Hallberg (RIP), Solene Oudet, Shaina Barnholt, Abner Mason, Waverly Gordon, Candace Montague, Chip Conley, Chris Hiller, Jan Nissen, Leslie Granese, Kedar Mate, Chris Jennings, Diana Lovett, Chris Brandt, Susan Holliday, Toyin Ajayi, Beverly Wasserman, Marcia Ellis, Victoria Silverman, Warren Ng, Carine Mathurin, Dave and Vicky Lane.

Thank you to the entire team at Grapevine Health who makes our work possible: Kat Kiyoko Amano, Samson Binutu, Josh Chamberlain, Nick Elias, Rachel Harbut, William Hoefle, Chinwendu Ngwadom, Randy Ray, Shamera Robinson, Fabian Sandoval, Neal Sikka and Tea Slater. And to the doctors who believe in the power of Grapevine Health and have joined us on the street and in executing Ask the Doctor programs: Yolandra Hancock, Dan Fagbuyi, Melissa Clarke and Tyson Bell.

Thank you also to our esteemed Advisory Board: Melissa Bradley, Christopher Brandt, Guillaume Castel, Jill DeGraff, Esther Dyson, Robert Hart, Aaron Leopold, René Quashie, Renata Simone and Vanessa Villaverde.

To seasoned healthcare experts who consistently support and give time to advise our leadership: Bill Georges, Chris Jennings, Abner Mason and Jon Stout.

Personal advisors and supporters: Lee Broome, Karen Dale, Shannah Koss, Jean Michel Mathurin and Sheryl Winarick.

The DC Community, including staff and leadership at Far Southeast Family and Strengthening Collaborative, United Planning Organization, Martha's Table and the Community Wellness Collective.

Harvard Kennedy School colleagues: Amy Davies, Mary Beaulieu, Amanda Peters, Carl Byers, Phyllis and Patrick Johnson, Nina Hernandez, Jonathan Fantini Porter, Vedette Gavin, Doug Gavel, Alexandra Martinez, Nicco Mele and Nick Stellitano.

My Aspen Health Innovator Fellow Cohort—The Justice League.

At Medicaid: Wayne Turnage, Claudia Schlosberg, Jean Michel Mathurin, Chris Jennings, Sheryl Winarick, Shannah Koss and Melissa Bradley.

Guillaume Castel, who has listened to and coached me every Friday for the last two years.

My professional advisors: Lee Broome, Chris Brandt, Esther Dyson, Renata Simone, Vanessa Sammy and Aaron Leopold.

My network of entrepreneurs and professional colleagues at Mindshare, Aspen Institute, Harvard, 1863 Ventures, The Modern Elder Academy and Alumni.

The National Academy of Medicine Roundtable on Health Literacy.

Thank you to Kate Broad at Broad Editorial for the writing support as I completed this book.

Appendix: Heard on the Street: Examples of Health Misconceptions and Misinformation

Can you do hookah when you're pregnant? My friend said it's not like cigarettes and won't hurt my baby.

Why do they draw so much blood? I felt like a lab rat.

The doctor told me because I was too old I had to test my baby. I didn't understand what she was saying. I was trying to figure out if she was telling me to get an abortion.

I don't go to the doctor because I ask them to test me for one thing and they always test me for something deeper.

Do you doctors understand how much stress you give people?

GW has an app but I can't use it. It's too complicated and there's too many passcodes.

Did you know certain places discriminate based on insurance?

Most of the doctors don't speak good English and I can't understand what they're saying.

I want to see the same doctor but every time I go it's somebody different.

I don't remember the doctors' names and I don't bother because it's always different.

It would be cool to have a Black doctor because other doctors think they're so much smarter than us—that we're stupid.

Foreign doctors think we're dumb and they rush through the visit trying to get you out. It was a waste of my time.

I don't like going to the doctor. Thinking about your body is kinda scary.

I'm not tryna go to a doctor unless I'm sick.

How do you know if you have cancer?

Does herpes lead to HIV?

What does it mean if I have a pain right here?

Once you start a medication you can never come off.

Once you have AIDS that's it, you die.

Does peeing on the ground give you a stye on your eye?

Walking outside with wet hair gives you walking pneumonia.

Bacon fat and ear wax can diagnose a sexually transmitted disease.

Index

Printed in the United States
by Baker & Taylor Publisher Services